The LLLove Story

The LLLove Story

By Kaye Lowman

Western U.S. Division
La Leche League International, Inc.
Franklin Park, Illinois

With heartfelt thanks to Mary Carson, who gave so generously of her talent and herself; and to Kay Kaszonyi, whose loving friendship made it all possible.

©1977 La Leche League International

TABLE OF CONTENTS

Infancy

- The Idea Is Conceived 9
- The Idea Is Born 11
- The Idea Takes Shape 12
- The Idea Becomes A Reality 15
- The Idea Is Refined 16
- The Idea Becomes La Leche League 18
- La Leche League
  - ... Reaches Out 18
  - ... Broadens Its Scope 21
  - ... Crystallizes Its Goal 22
  - ... Realizes Baby Knows Best 22
  - ... Writes A Book 23
  - ... Issues A Newsletter 25
  - ... Becomes Incorporated 27
  - ... Formalizes Its Organization 27
  - ... Expands Its Lines Of Communication 28
  - ... Loses A Founder To Denver ... 29
  - ... Hires Its First Employee 30
  - ... Rents Its First Office 30
  - ... Receives Public Recognition ... 31

Growing Up

- Writing a "Real" Book 35
- Beginning To Organize Its Leaders 37
- Finding A Symbol 38
- Writing A Constitution 40
- Formulating A Statement Of Policy 40
- Becoming International 41
- Holding A Convention 41
- Appointing An Executive Coordinator 43
- Appointing A Director Of New Group Chairmen 44
- Expanding Its Office Space 45
- Issuing A Leaders' Publication 50
- Moving ... Again 50
- Gathering In Indianapolis 51
- ... And Again In Denver 51
- Raising The Roof 52
- Forming The LLLI Committee 52
- Being Charmed By A Princess 53
- Appointing A Public Relations Director .. 54
- Publishing A Cookbook 55
- Keeping Up With The Mail 55
- Expanding The Professional Advisory Board 56
- The Printed Words Flow On 57
- Continuing To Answer The Need For Breastfeeding Help 58

La Leche League Comes of Age

- La Leche League
  - ... Recognizes The Need For A New Governing Structure 61
  - ... Clarifies Its Philosophy 61
  - ... Develops A Human Relations Training Program 62
  - ... Initiates Information Service Centers 63
  - ... Holds Physicians' Seminars ... 64
  - ... Fills The Need For A Teaching Film 65
  - ... Establishes A Liaison With The Medical Community 66
  - ... Develops Research Guidelines 66
  - ... Convenes In Chicago 67
  - ... Reorganizes Into Divisions 69
  - ... Writes A Leader's Handbook .. 70
  - ... Expands Its Reference Library 71
  - ... Looks For Funding 71
  - ... Works With Friends And Relatives 71
- In The Years To Come 74

The Seven Speak for Themselves

- The Cahills 76
- The Froehlichs 78
- The Kerwins 80
- The Lennons 82
- The Tompsons 84
- The Wagners 86
- The Whites 88
- A Postscript To The Reader 91

La Leche League's First - And Foremost - Medical Advisors 46

Drawings on pages 4 and 11 and the back cover by Joy Sidor, who illustrated THE WOMANLY ART OF BREASTFEEDING.

In the 1950s

- Formula was providing scientifically perfect food for babies
- Anesthesia was saving mothers from the horrors of childbirth
- Bottles were making it easy for anyone to care for the baby
- Schedules and discipline from the moment of birth were preventing babies from ruling their parents' lives

In 1956, seven women joined together in a movement that was to change the face of motherhood in America. They have devoted their lives to bringing mother and baby together again.

This is their story.

 Mary Ann Kerwin

 Mary White

 Edwina Froehlich

 Viola Lennon

 Betty Wagner

 Mary Ann Cahill

 Marian Tompson

In this 1957 photo, Marian with Sheila on her lap and Laurel beside her, and Mary Ann Kerwin with Tommy and baby Eddie, look over a copy of Grantly Dick-Read's *Childbirth Without Fear*.

LaVerne Bollig, left, holding the original loose leaf version of THE WOMANLY ART OF BREASTFEEDING, helps Edwina compose personal letters sent out with every manual.

Infancy

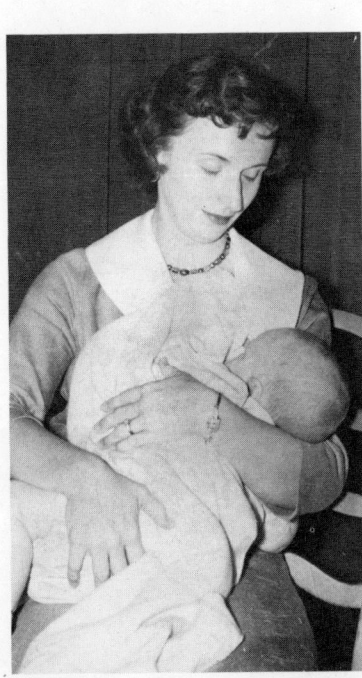

Marian with Brian in 1959 photo that appeared on the cover of *Herald of Health* magazine, and later in *Time* magazine.

A 1963 League meeting at Betty Wagner's home. Betty is in the back row between the picture display and the lamp, with Edwina in the dark dress in front of her. Betty Cummings is seated in the chair at the far right. Marybeth Doucette is standing in the back row at the far left.

The Idea Is Conceived

It was 1949 when young Dr. Gregory White finished his residency and was looking for a place to set up his medical practice. He decided on Franklin Park, Illinois, a suburb on the western outskirts of Chicago. It was a community that was attracting many young families with its industry, low taxes, and new housing, and seemed to be a good location for a new doctor who wanted to establish a family practice.

Dr. White found office space on Franklin Avenue in Franklin Park, and the Whites—Greg, Mary, and young sons Joe and Bill — settled into a big old house a few blocks away on Gustave Street.

While he was a student at Loyola Medical School, Greg White's teacher and mentor, Dr. Herbert Ratner, became one of the dominant influences in his life. Dr. Ratner imparted to the young Dr. White an abiding faith in the wisdom of nature which Greg reflected both in his practice of medicine and in his home.

"Greg had always said to me, 'Naturally you are going to nurse our babies,' and I had always said, 'Of course, naturally, I will,'" Mary White recalled.

But Greg was in the Army on a ship transporting British war brides to the United States when the Whites' first baby was born in 1945.

"He was home for the delivery and a few days after and then went back to his bride ship," Mary said. "Joe was so full of drugs from the delivery that he didn't know how to nurse for two days. Then we went home to live with my mother, who was very bottle and schedule oriented. I supplemented because they told me at the hospital that I didn't have enough milk, so Joe soon became strictly a bottle baby."

Soon after Joe was born, Greg had a weekend furlough in New York, and Mary and the baby joined him there for the weekend. Baby Joe was sleeping soundly in their room when they were ready to go downstairs to the hotel dining room for dinner. The young parents were uncertain what to do, but finally decided to leave the baby and go downstairs and eat.

"An old German waiter saw us and asked where the baby was," Mary recalled. "When we told him we had left the baby in our room he was horrified. 'You go right back upstairs and get that baby!' he told us. I had been worried about leaving Joe alone and was so relieved to be told that the right thing to do was to go and get him."

Greg was out of the Army before Bill was born eighteen months later, and he had come across Grantly Dick-Read's *Childbirth without Fear*.

"The obstetrician we were going to had never heard of natural childbirth," Mary recalled, "but we decided to try it anyway. Greg was allowed in the delivery room because he was a doctor, and with us warding off the anesthetists at one end and the doctor at the other we managed to have a natural delivery.

"We decided that this time around we would give the nursing a really good try," Mary said, "and now that Greg was home he could give me lots of encouragement. I was convinced that I was going to be a complete failure because I had been the first time, but it all worked out and we never had another bottle in the house."

The Whites' third child, Peggy, was born in the spring of 1949 and was the last of their children to be born in the hospital.

"My doctor was going to be out of town when the fourth baby was due," Mary said. "Greg suggested that we just stay home this time and let our good friend Herb Ratner come over and assist with the birth. Everything worked out beautifully and we decided that was the way we wanted to have all the rest of our babies."

Though busy with her young family, Mary found time to participate in other activities. She was attending a meeting the night she and Betty Wagner met.

"I was at a meeting where a book review was being given," Betty recalled, "and the lady who was giving the review said a word that was strange to me and asked if anyone knew the meaning of the word. Way in the back of the hall Mary White's hand went up. There were a lot of people there and she was the only one in the hall who thought she knew what it meant — and she did! I thought that anybody like that was worth knowing, so after the meeting I went over and talked with her. She had just moved into town, so I started introducing her around and we became friends."

Edwina Froehlich is fond of telling that Mary was barefoot and pregnant when they met. The

Mary with Joseph, three months old, 1945.

Froehlichs were house hunting in 1952 and one of the houses they were interested in was in Franklin Park. Edwina was a patient of Dr. White's, and knowing that he lived in Franklin Park she decided to see where his house was in relation to the one she and her husband were considering buying.

"It was early on a summer evening," Edwina recalled. "When we drove up Mary was standing on the front porch, pregnant and in shorts and bare feet, with little kids all around. It was a hot, muggy summer night, and she had just hosed down the front porch. We trooped up the wet stairs and into her house and sat and got acquainted."

John and Edwina Froehlich bought the Franklin Park house. The Froehlichs and the Whites were all active members of St. Gertrude's Catholic Church, and a short time later Mary invited the Froehlichs to attend a couples program at church. Mary offered to send over a friend who had three children and was a "nice mama-type" to babysit for Edwina's two boys. The babysitter turned out to be Marian Tompson.

Marian became a patient of Dr. White's in 1954 before the birth of her fourth baby. Her first three births had been unmedicated but not very satisfying because of the hospital's routine and the attitude of the staff. Marian's attempts at breastfeeding had been similarly dissatisfying. Each time she had been told she didn't have enough milk and had put the babies on the bottle.

"Edwina is fond of telling that Mary White was barefoot and pregnant when they met."

"I belonged to a Christian Family Movement group," Marian said, "and before I had my fourth baby someone in my group told me there was a doctor in one of the other CFM groups who would deliver babies at home. I had so wanted my husband to be with me for the births of our babies, but husbands weren't allowed in the delivery room. I was regarded as a novelty at the hospital because I had my babies naturally. When I went to the hospital to have my second baby they took me right into the delivery room. I couldn't believe it—everyone was there — externs, interns, even my doctor's receptionist had closed the office so she could see the birth. A natural delivery was a new thing, and they all wanted to see it. People were swarming all around the delivery table. I gave three pushes and there was the baby. My hair was still in place and my lipstick was still on, and one of the doctors, with awe in his voice, turned to my doctor and said, 'Doctor, how did you do it!' He had seen it and he didn't even know what he had seen."

To Marian and husband Tom's delight, Dr. White delivered their fourth baby at home. Dr. White also provided Marian with the breastfeeding support she needed, and she was able to successfully nurse baby Laurel.

Though basically a quiet person, Marian had a way of holding out for what she wanted and believed was right. Betty Wagner had discovered that when she met Marian in 1952.

"I was working as an election judge," Betty said. "Marian came in to vote and she had two little girls with her, a little blonde and a brunette. This was her first time to vote, and she was all set to do it. But she wasn't registered! I was the judge, and I said, 'If you are not registered, you can't vote.'

"It was their love for mothers and babies everywhere that gave birth to their idea."

"Marian replied, 'Oh, but I *am* registered. I made a special trip downtown to do it, and I know that I am registered.'

"'Well,' I said, 'we don't have your name on our official list and we have to have it listed in order for you to vote.'

"'Well,' Marian said, 'I know I registered. Will you please check it out further?'

"She was very pregnant," Betty said, "and standing there with these two little girls, and I felt sorry for her, so I said, 'Well, I can send someone to call downtown to see if they have your name on file, but it could take qute a bit of time.'

"Marian said, 'Please call downtown, I'll wait.'

"One call would refer us someplace else, so we had to make several calls and it did take quite a long while. She sat there all that time with those two little girls, waiting patiently. The girls weren't very old, only about one and two. Finally the message came back. They had found her name officially listed so we could allow her to vote. So, happily, Marian finally got to vote. I was eventually to learn that that's exactly the way Marian is. If she knows she's right, she won't let you brush her aside. We got to talking while she sat there and I discovered that she only lived a couple of blocks from me and that we were active in the same church. We saw a lot of each other after that."

Marian recalled that before she actually met Mary White she had heard many people say what a wonderful mother Mary was.

"I was asked to do a panel at church on parenting, and because of what I had heard about Mary I called her up and asked her if she would be on the panel with me," Marian said. "She agreed, and when we sat next to each other at the program I got my first introduction to unobtrusive nursing. She was holding the baby, and when I heard this 'slurp, slurp' I realized she was nursing the baby. I never knew you could nurse in public like that without anyone being able to see what you were doing."

Once they became acquainted, Mary and Marian quickly became close friends. It was their friendship and philosophy that drew them together. It was their love for mothers and babies everywhere that gave birth to their idea.

The Idea Is Born

It was hot and sunny that July day in 1956. A perfect day for the Christian Family Movement picnic that Mary White and Marian Tompson were planning to attend with their families. Neither of them could guess that before the day was over they would make a decision whose impact would be felt across the country and around the world.

Mary had happily breastfed all but the first of her six children. Marian, at last, was successfully nursing her fourth baby. Both women had friends who would see them happily nursing their babies and express regret that they had been unable to nurse their own. Mary and Marian felt certain they could have helped these mothers, had they only known these mothers needed help before it was too late. For many months they had been thinking that something should be done to keep this from happening over and over again. But what?

The idea was born at a picnic.

For some time Marian had been giving a great deal of thought to finding a way to be of help to other mothers. Originally she had been interested in forming an organization to help mothers have unmedicated deliveries. But Dr. White had pointed out to her that for most women childbirth was always going to be a medical event, taking place in a hospital under medical supervision. Besides, Margaret Gamper, who was a nurse, was already providing childbirth classes for mothers. He suggested, instead, that she think about doing something to help women who wanted to nurse their babies. He pointed out to her that breastfeeding was a nonmedical situation and that mothers did it in their homes rather than in hospitals. And, Dr. White pointed out, no one was offering any help to nursing mothers. It was an interesting idea, and Marian had been turning it over in her mind.

> *"Before the day was over, they would make a decision whose impact would be felt across the country and around the world."*

As she and Mary relaxed under a tree at the picnic at Wilder Park in Elmhurst, Illinois, they saw mothers worrying over trying to keep bottles chilled and then trying to heat them for their babies, and they commented to each other how lucky they were to be nursing mothers. Mary and Marian both knew firsthand about bottle feeding babies, and they were grateful that they were enjoying the ease and convenience of nursing.

"It's a shame more mothers don't nurse," Mary remarked to Marian.

As Mary nursed baby number six, Jeannie, she and Marian sat chatting under the tree. Throughout the afternoon, one by one and in groups, mothers at the picnic walked over to them and said, "I had so wanted to nurse my baby, but..."

"That's when it really hit us that the problems we had had in trying to nurse our babies were common to a lot of other mothers," Marian recalled. "It wasn't just Mary's particular rare problem or my particular rare problem."

They could see that nearly every one of those mothers would have been able to nurse her baby if she had had the help she needed. Mary and Marian had learned the art of breastfeeding by trial and error. Though Dr. White had had little practical information to offer, they realized what a tremendous help his support and encouragement had been. It was his confidence in their ability to nurse and his assurance that their babies were thriving that had enabled them to successfully breastfeed their babies.

Mary and Marian felt that they now knew the secrets of a successful nursing experience—information and encouragement. They agreed that they knew far too many mothers who were getting neither and were therefore unable to nurse their babies. Then and there they decided to do what they could to help their friends in the community who wanted to nurse their babies.

They saw the need, and they decided to try to fill it.

The Idea Takes Shape

Edwina Froehlich recalls vividly the call she got from Marian the day after the picnic.

"You know how we've been talking about wanting to help other nursing mothers?" Marian asked. "Well, Mary and I have decided that we're just going to start. We don't know exactly what we're going to do, but we're going to have to start somewhere. We're going to have a meeting at Mary's house next week. Come if you're interested, and if you know anyone else that you think would be interested, bring her along."

Edwina *was* interested. She had long believed that the natural way was the best way to do most things in life. Not only had she successfully breastfed her two boys, but she was the first of his patients that Dr. White had delivered at home.

Edwina had become a patient of Dr. White's in 1950 when her doctor, Dr. Herbert Ratner, phased out his practice and turned over many of his patients to his friend and former student, Greg White. Dr. White provided Edwina with the encouragement that enabled her to nurse her children. Edwina provided Dr. White with the opportunity to

> *"I made a big to-do about my labor," Edwina recalled. "I could be ashamed of myself if I wanted to."*

see whether home births were a viable alternative for his patients.

"When I became pregnant, Dr. White gave me Grantly Dick-Read's book to read," Edwina recalled. "When I read it I was so excited. I said to myself, 'That's it!' I wanted to have my baby at home, too, just like the women in the book."

The Whites had recently had their first home birth experience when their fourth child, Katie, was born at home, and felt that it offered tremendous advantages over a hospital birth. Were there other women who would like this very special birth experience, too? Dr. White didn't know and wasn't sure how he could find out.

Having no idea what was going on in Dr. White's mind, Edwina finally gathered up enough courage to bring up the subject of a home birth with him.

Edwina recalled, "With fear and trepidation I said to him, 'What would be my chances be of having this baby at home?'

"He said, 'Well, very good, in fact,' and I nearly dropped dead!"

While Edwina was delighted at the prospect of having her baby born at home, other people were horrified.

"I had family, distant relatives, call me and tell me what a risk I was taking," Edwina said. "People I didn't even know were friends were calling me and telling me not to do it. One relative said to me, 'Edwina, that man is right out of the dark ages! He's a horse and buggy man!' And another relative sat me down sternly and said, 'This cannot be! You can't go through with this!'"

Friends were all but placing bets on at what point husband John would pass out, but Dr. White assured her that he would rise to the occasion.

Both Dr. White and Dr. Ratner were present for Edwina's labor and delivery.

"I made a big to-do about my labor," Edwina recalled. "I could be ashamed of myself if I wanted to. I was in such a state emotionally that John had to calm me down to get me to cooperate with the doctor. He would say, 'Come on, we're going to do it together — we're going to do it together.' He was like a coach even though there were no classes to attend back then where husbands were told they were supposed to be birth coaches. It was just like Dr. White had said it would be. It was obvious I was depending on him, and he was responding to my needs."

Baby Paul was born at 4 a.m.

"After it was over, John got very glassy-eyed and went to bed," Edwina said. "He was snoring when my mother rang the doorbell at seven, so I went to answer the door. My mother's eyes nearly popped right out of her head! She shouted, 'Where in God's name is your husband?' and I said, 'Shh. He's in bed sleeping.'"

Yes, Edwina was certainly interested in Marian's idea. She loved to share her experiences and her philosophy with anyone who would listen, as Betty Wagner found out the night that she and Edwina met.

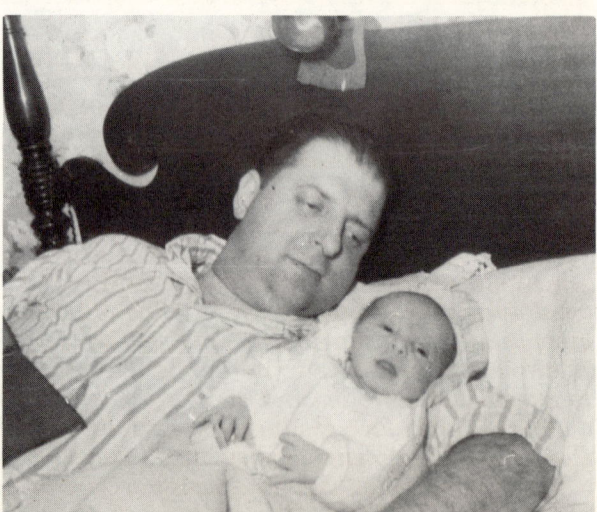

Daddy John Froehlich with three week old Paul, 1950.

"I was driving some friends to a ladies guild meeting," Betty recalled, "and one of them asked me if I would pick up this new arrival in town who wanted to attend the meeting. It was Edwina who got in the car, and the subject soon turned to childbirth. Edwina started telling us about her childbirth experience, how she had had her baby at home and had nursed him.

"This fascinated me," Betty recalled. "I didn't know anyone except my mother who had had a

"Betty laughed at the idea of a club for nursing mothers, but she said she'd come."

baby at home. Everything she said I agreed with. All evening I listened intently as Edwina talked. She was so vivacious and interesting. I just ate up everything she said. I thought, 'Oh, this marvelous woman!'

"After we dropped Edwina off at her house," Betty said, "my friend said, 'Wasn't she AWFUL!' I was so shocked! I had been so interested and my friend had been bored to death! I thought, 'My goodness. One of us has to be wrong!' That was the beginning of the end of that friendship, and the beginning of my friendship with Edwina."

Not only did Edwina want to join the group, but she knew someone else who she was sure would be interested, too.

Edwina's friendship with Viola Lennon went back some ten years. They had become acquainted when both were involved in the Young Christian Workers, a Catholic organization for single people dedicated to bringing about social change and providing what is now called consciousness raising for its members. In the beginning Edwina had volunteered her spare time, but in 1946, she decided that the need was so great that she quit a lucrative

"Just by being what she was, Mary was an example to us all."

job with a management engineering firm to become the YCW's first national president. There was no salary to go with the job, so Edwina relied on donations to support herself and her mother.

Vi Lennon had come into the YCW while still in college, during the time Edwina was national president, and the two had become close friends as they worked together.

Shortly after she graduated, fate brought Vi under Dr. Ratner's influence.

"I was taking some classes at Catholic University in Washington, D.C., in the summer of 1948," Vi said. "A priest introduced me to Dr. Ratner, who was there for a seminar. I liked his philosophy and he became both my friend and my doctor."

By the time Vi married and became pregnant, Dr. Ratner had become Health Commissioner of Oak Park, Illinois, and was turning his patients over to Dr. White. All of Vi's children were born naturally with Dr. White in attendance, and all were breast-fed.

"When Edwina called and asked if I'd like to join the group, I was flattered, but I wanted to know more," Vi remembered. "I knew a lot about nursing babies, but Edwina mentioned 'mothering.' I wasn't quite sure what that meant and I wanted to know more about it."

Vi made quite an impression on the group when they all met together for the first time at Mary's house.

"The first time I met Viola was when we formed the group," Betty Wagner recalled. "Edwina had told me about Viola, but I wasn't prepared for SEEING Viola! She looked like she had just stepped out of *Mademoiselle*. She came into a room in a very self-possessed way that I both envied and enjoyed. She had the knack of attributing much more knowledge to people than they actually had. She made you feel good about yourself, as if you were really important. You're naturally glad to have her, and she naturally ASSUMES that you're glad to have her, and so you are! She seemed so full of wisdom and made you feel that she could solve any

"I knew a lot about nursing babies, but Edwina mentioned 'mothering.' I wasn't quite sure what that meant."

problem that might arise."

Mary White had two friends in mind for the group. She called her sister-in-law, Mary Ann Kerwin, who had breastfed her first baby and was expecting her second.

"It was only through the Whites' help that I was able to breastfeed Tommy," Mary Ann recalled, "so I was eager to do what I could to help other mothers in the way I had been helped. I also liked the idea of having discussions with other breastfeeding women from whom I could learn and exchange information and ideas."

Betty Wagner remembers her first impression of Mary Ann Kerwin.

"I met Mary Ann for the first time when we got together to form the group," Betty recalled. "She was very young and was nursing her first baby, who was still very little. Everything she said was so nice and thoughtful of other people. At first I wondered how anyone could be that nice, but I soon learned that Mary Ann's sweetness was completely sincere."

Mary also placed a call to Mary Ann Cahill. They

had become acquainted through their involvement with the Christian Family Movement.

"Mary Ann and I hit it off right away," Mary recalled. "Not only were we both nursing mothers, but we felt the same way about families and children and had the same philosophy of life. I knew that Mary Ann would be a natural for the group."

Mary Ann's response to the invitation to join the group was immediate and enthusiastic.

"I didn't have to think about whether or not this was the right thing to do," Mary Ann recalled. "I thought, 'Of course! This is exactly what I needed with my first babies. Let's get together and help other mothers so they won't have the problems that I did.' I welcomed the idea of joining a group where we could help other mothers and discuss breastfeeding."

Mary Ann had had a difficult time nursing her first baby, and it was with Betty Wagner's help that she was able to successfully breastfeed her second.

Betty remembers meeting Mary Ann and how satisfying it was to be able to help her nurse her baby.

"Mary Ann came and knocked on my door one day," Betty said. "She was taking a survey for our church. I was flabbergasted! There were only about three thousand people living in Franklin Park, and I thought I knew everybody. Yet here was this

"Then Mary White said, 'Listen, Marian, this was really your idea. You've got to be president.' I was really rather quiet and shy, so I didn't object."

stranger taking a survey for MY church! She said she had just moved into town and she worked on the assumption that if you wanted to get acquainted, you had to get out and do things. So when she had gone to the church to register she had asked if there was anything she could do, and they said yes, take this survey.

"She had little red-headed Elizabeth in the stroller with her," Betty recalled, "and she said, 'Why don't you come with me and we'll do the rest of the survey together?' So I went. I found out that she hadn't been able to nurse Elizabeth for very long, so when she got pregnant with her second baby I offered advice based on what I had learned from nursing my own, and I felt so good when she was able to nurse Tim."

So when Mary White asked Mary Ann Cahill to join the group and bring along any interested friends, Mary Ann immediately thought of Betty.

"She was the one who had been so helpful to me," Mary Ann said, "so I asked her if she would like to join the group. I remember how Betty laughed at the idea of a club for nursing mothers, but she said she'd come."

So these seven women, Marian Tompson, Mary White, Edwina Froehlich, Viola Lennon, Betty Wagner, Mary Ann Kerwin, and Mary Ann Cahill, comprised the original group and became the founding mothers of La Leche League. They were all women who had overcome difficulties and successfully breastfed their babies. And they all saw the need to provide help for nursing mothers and enthusiastically supported Mary and Marian's plan.

They met together several times during the summer and early fall to make plans for their group. They began by trying to isolate the reasons mothers failed at breastfeeding and what they needed to succeed. They knew from their own experience that prime worries for nursing mothers

"Talking about the early days of the League without talking about Greg and Mary White would be like trying to paint The Blue Boy without any blue."

were fears that they didn't have enough milk or that their milk wasn't "right" for their baby. Mary borrowed her husband's medical books and they gathered all the information they could find, though there was precious little.

"We went through all the material we could find," Mary Ann Cahill said. "We kept coming back to the idea that nature hadn't left women high and dry—they had been left with milk for their babies."

"I remember so well those early organizational meetings at the Whites' house," Mary Ann said. "We sat around exchanging nursing experiences and expressing to each other what breastfeeding meant to us and how really important it was in our lives. It was something we already knew, but in telling it it was intensified. Just finding kindred spirits was in itself a kind of high.

"I remember how Dr. White used to come in after he'd finished with his office hours," Mary Ann continued, "and sit and talk with us. Seven mothers would only have been seven mothers without his professional guidance. We looked to him for the answers we needed. He had long ago recognized the importance of mother-to-mother help in breastfeeding and had had it going informally in his practice for quite a while. When he had a new nursing mother he would say, 'I know so-and-so who lives in your neighborhood and has nursed a couple of babies. Why don't you call her up? I know she would have lots of practical tips for you.' He recognized that one woman needed another."

Mary Ann feels it would be impossible to overestimate the importance of the Whites' contributions to the formation of La Leche League.

"We would have never gotten off the ground without them," Mary Ann said. "Talking about the early days of the League without talking about

14

Greg and Mary White would be like trying to paint The Blue Boy without any blue.

"I will never forget those early sessions at their home. Mary had an older and larger family than most of the rest of us and was much further advanced in her mothering. She had strength, confidence, and sureness and combined it with ability. Her singlemindedness on the importance of mothering was such an influence on us. Just by being what she was, Mary was an example to us all."

Even though they were a small group with modest intentions, the founding mothers decided that they should have officers.

"I suggested Edwina for president because she seemed like a very executive-type lady," Marian said. "But she said, 'Oh, no. I don't want to be president.'

"Then Mary White said, 'Listen, Marian, this was really your idea. You've got to be president.' I was really a rather quiet and shy person, so I didn't object," Marian said. "The job didn't seem like it would be too difficult."

"Actually, we voted her in while she was out of the room," Mary White said.

Vi Lennon became vice president. Edwina Froehlich, who had long years of experience as a secretary, was the obvious choice for that post. Little did she realize how big that job would become in almost no time at all.

"Betty Wagner said she had been treasurer of every group she ever belonged to, so she enthusiastically accepted the job of treasurer," Mary Ann Kerwin said. "At that time we had no money and no apparent need for much, so that job didn't look like much of a burden.

"I offered to be librarian," Mary Ann Kerwin said, "because I loved to read and had read every bit of information on breastfeeding then available through the Whites' unofficial lending library.

"Right from the start," Mary Ann continued, "Mary White was our liaison with the medical profession. And Mary Ann Cahill was our unequalled writer."

So with each founding mother contributing her own special talent, the infant La Leche League was ready to be born.

The Idea Becomes A Reality

At 8:45 on an October evening in 1956, the first La Leche League meeting was held at Mary White's home at 2932 Gustave Street, Franklin Park, Illinois. Since Mary was kept busy answering the doorbell and telephone and caring for her six small children, it fell to Marian to lead the first meetings.

The first meeting was attended by the seven founding mothers and five of their pregnant friends. The founding mothers had very little idea how to go about giving these women the help they needed, but they were determined to try. They were very certain about what they wanted to accomplish — they wanted to give individual, mother-to-mother help to their friends who wanted to nurse their babies.

"I began the meeting by doing something I would never advise anyone to do now," Marian recalled. "I read 'Breast Fed Is Best Fed' from *Reader's Digest* to the group so we could discuss it."

Whether it was the best approach or not, the mothers responded enthusiastically to the warmth and caring that they found at Mary White's house that night.

"I remember very well being so excited after that first meeting," Edwina recalled. "I could see that it had such great possibilities, although I wondered where we were going to get the information we needed. There was practically nothing in print at the time.

"It was so obvious that we were giving them the support and encouragement that we had gotten from our doctor (Dr. White) that had helped us to be successful," Edwina said. "They were responding to our support, and it was a feeling of, 'Isn't it wonderful we've all found each other!'"

"We only set out to help our friends, people we knew," Marian explained. "We never put an ad in the paper or anything like that. That's why it was such a surprise to us when women we didn't know

The Whites' home, where the first La Leche League meeting was held in 1956.

started coming to the door. We weren't thinking in terms of helping the whole town."

Not only were the meetings filling a void for the prospective nursing mothers, but they were serving an important function for the founding mothers as well.

"The meetings did so much for me," Edwina reminisced. "They confirmed everything for me, put everything into words. I had a lot of inner feelings about babies and breastfeeding, and I hadn't had another mother to share them with. None of us who founded the League had ever before really shared with each other the depth of our feelings about breastfeeding and mothering until we got together at the first meeting.

"The meetings were reinforcing, removing the last vestiges of doubt, broadening my thinking," she said. "It is so important to find someone who shares an important feeling with you. When something is really important to you, you want to share it with someone else who thinks it's important, too. That's what made the League work."

And work it did. Not a handful of friends, but thirty and forty women, most of them strangers, crowded into the meetings. Within only a few months there were so many women asking to come that it was necessary to split into two groups.

Mary and Marian had seen the need and had begun to fill it. It was an idea whose time had come.

The Idea Is Refined

The early meetings were loosely structured as the founding mothers worked to learn how they could be most helpful to these women who wanted to nurse their babies. They simply proceeded from meeting to meeting giving their personal help and encouragement to mothers who wanted it and learned through trial and error how they could make their help most effective.

One of the earliest decisions they made was to refer to themselves as "leaders."

"We thought 'counselor' sounded too professional and would be misleading," Marian explained.

"Most of us had been affiliated with other organizations that had small groups with discussion leaders," Edwina said. "The term 'leader' was very commonly used. Anybody who was leading a discussion group was called a group leader."

So the seven founding mothers decided to call themselves leaders.

After several months they had enough experience behind them to arrive at an organizational structure that they felt would best serve the mothers' needs.

They started out with a series of four meetings, including a fathers' meeting, and met every three weeks.

"We hit on starting out with the advantages," Mary Ann Cahill explained. "That just seemed right. Then we wanted to cover the common concerns—the old wives' tales. Of course, there had to be the how-to.

"Then it became apparent that we had to include something on childbirth, even though to a lot of women childbirth and breastfeeding were entirely separate questions," Mary Ann said. "We believed that the relationship between a mother and baby begins at birth. We tried to tie the two together. We wanted them to see that mothering begins as soon as the baby is born and put to the breast."

"In that era a women's body was pretty much unknown to her," Betty explained. "We had pregnant women coming who had no idea how they were going to deliver the baby."

"So many mothers who came who were expecting babies were petrified," Marian said. "They had had several babies and had been knocked out and were afraid of the whole thing. The seven of us were all having our babies naturally, so when these women would come and be so fearful and not know what it was all about, we were surprised because all of us had had such a different kind of experience."

After using a four-meeting series for a short time, a meeting on nutrition was added.

"We got into the nutritional aspects of breastfeeding when we noticed that the mothers were losing their milk because of starting solids early," Marian explained.

"We all studied up on nutrition," Mary Ann Kerwin said. "We learned and taught all we could about easy, sensible, good nutrition."

There was also a keen interest in nutrition, Mary Ann Cahill explained, because there were so many old wives' tales associated with what a nursing mother could and could not eat.

"There wasn't an acceptance of and interest in good nutrition in the fifties like there is now, but we realized that the mothers would feel better and so would be better mothers if they ate well," Mary Ann Cahill said.

So the founding mothers settled on a five-meeting series and invited mothers to join them for one series. With each new series, they would begin again with a new group of mothers.

The first manual, printed in 1958, offered the following description of the series of meetings:

Their purpose is to explain, discuss and advise on breastfeeding to a living room full of interested mothers (and most welcome, but not always so interested babies), grandmothers, et al.

A series of five meetings has been worked out which points out the advantages of breastfeeding to mother and baby; explains the necessary how-to of nursing; discusses weaning and the baby in relation to the rest of the family; suggests good procedure during pregnancy and at the time of delivery; takes a stab at promoting really good nutrition for the nursing mother (and the rest of the family, too, of course). Even father comes into his own at a special For Fathers Only meeting conducted by a nationally-known speaker on marriage and the family. Then the series is finished, the mothers graduate, and three new groups start another series.*

It was the fifth meeting of the series that was for fathers, and it was led by Dr. Herbert Ratner. Dr. Ratner became involved in the League through his close friendship with the Whites. Children and parents had long been his special interest, and as Health Commissioner of Oak Park, Illinois, he conducted parent forums that enjoyed tremendous popularity. His background and his relationship with the Whites inevitably drew him into the League. When the founding mothers decided that they wanted to make a fathers' meeting part of their series, he was the natural choice to lead it.

"We felt the fathers' meeting was very important because we realized from the beginning that fathers weren't getting any support," Marian explained.

"We knew fathers were very important persons who at that time were too often neglected as far as babies were concerned," Mary Ann Kerwin added.

"In the beginning, we had a lot of trouble getting the husbands to go," Edwina recalled. "Then it got so some of the League fathers would call up some of the new men and say, 'I'll pick you up at 8:00. It's no trouble. You're right on my way. We can relax over a couple of beers.' That went a long way toward breaking the ice for the men who were new to the group."

Some wives used the technique of "I'll tell my husband your husband is going, and you tell your husband my husband is going," Mary White said. "The fathers were skeptical, but they wound up loving it. We had good crowds at the fathers' meetings."

"I remember once we had a fathers' meeting at my house," Edwina said. "We women really bent over backwards to make ourselves scarce. I simply brought in the food and disappeared. But I had the ironing board set up in the kitchen, and I was as close to the door as I could get so I could hear the questions they were asking!

"Dr. Ratner would say, 'Now what is really important in life? It's not having a spotless house so your mother can come over and inspect. It's your kids that are important,'" Edwina recalled.

"The fathers came away from the meeting with an understanding of a wife's new role as a mother and of her special attachment to the baby," Betty said. "Dr. Ratner helped them feel good about having the baby in bed with them. It was important for the father to hear these things, because he wasn't hearing it anyplace else."

At the conclusion of one of the early fathers' meetings, a satisfied participant was heard to remark, "Think how much this would have cost us if we consulted privately with a doctor for three hours. We got it all for nothing!"

---

*There were only two groups at the end of the year, but a third group had been formed in Chicago by the time the manual was written.

The founding mothers, 1957 — Mary Ann Cahill with Mary; Betty Wagner with Peggy; Mary Ann Kerwin with Tommy and baby Eddie; Mary White with Michael; Marian Tompson with Laurel and Sheila; Edwina Froehlich with Peter. Only Vi Lennon escaped the camera.

The Idea Becomes La Leche League

No one was more surprised than the founding mothers that so many women were hungry for the breastfeeding information and support that they were offering. Because their ambition for their group was so limited, and the popularity of the group so unexpected, they didn't even get around to naming their group until early in 1957, after it had been in existence for several months.

"Our husbands kept teasing us with all kinds of names for our organization," Edwina recalled. "They called us 'The Bust Ladies' and 'The Milk Maids,' and we decided we had to find a name for ourselves to put an end to their teasing."

But finding a suitable name presented quite a problem. "In those days you didn't mention 'breast' in print unless you were talking about Jean Harlow," Edwina explained. The founders realized that they needed to find a socially acceptable name for their group.

"We knew that if we were ever going to get anything in the paper we would have to find a name that wouldn't actually tell people what our organization was about," Edwina said. "You couldn't print anything in the newspaper about breasts, and we didn't want people to be embarrassed to get mail with the name of our organization on it."

It was Dr. White who finally suggested the name of La Leche League. He was in the habit of giving a medal of the shrine of the Spanish Madonna, *Nuestra Senora de La Leche y Buen Parto**, in St. Augustine, Florida, to his patients when they became pregnant. The founding mothers realized that only those in the know would understand what "La Leche" referred to, and no one would be embarrassed. They quickly agreed that the name "La Leche League" was just what the doctor ordered!

*Freely translated, "Our Lady of Happy Delivery and Plentiful Milk."

La Leche League...Reaches Out

When the founding mothers realized after the first few League meetings that many women in addition to their personal friends wanted help nursing their babies, they decided that a pamphlet explaining their organization and its purpose was in order.

The first brochure, issued in 1957, was titled, "For Better Mothers." It explained the reasons the League was formed, its purpose, and the series of meetings.

By the time they issued the second pamphlet in 1958, the founding mothers realized that the title of the first brochure had implied that breastfeeding mothers were "better" mothers. So the pamphlet was retitled "Your Baby and You." It offered more detailed information about the League, its meetings, and its objectives: "La Leche ... means life, love and the beginning of happiness to a baby. This is the concern of La Leche."

It was with the third edition of the brochure in 1959 that the title "Why Nurse Your Baby" was used. As a result of the meeting with Dr. Ratner where the founding mothers realized the importance of the mothering philosophy they offered, a

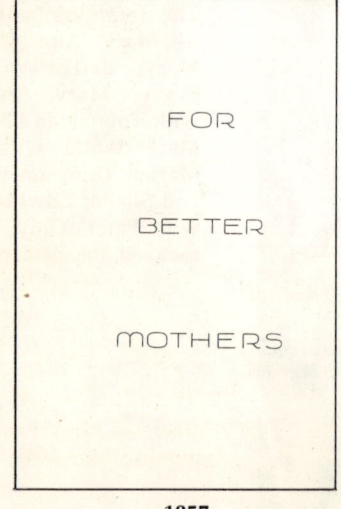

1957

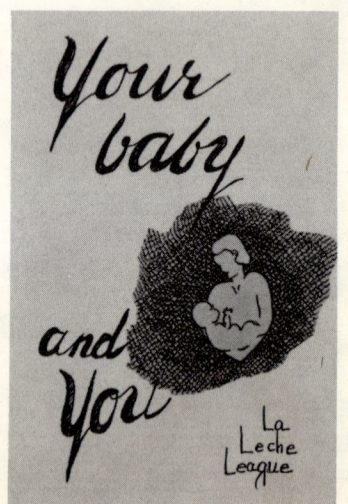

1958

18

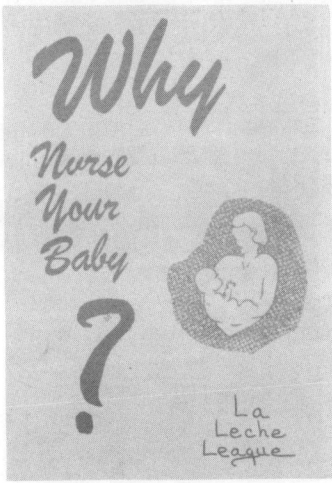
1959

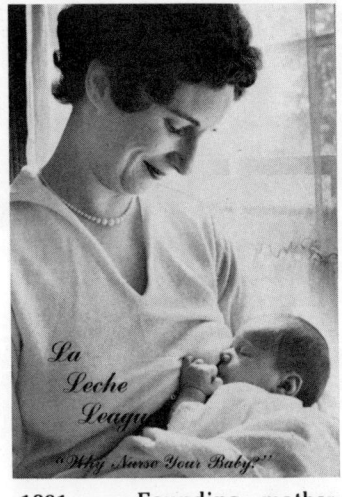
1961 — Founding mother Betty Wagner with Helen.

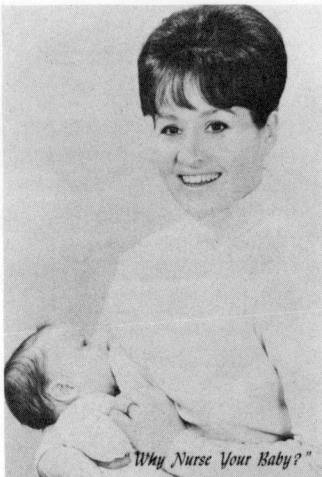
1965 — Mrs. Robert Troch nursing her third baby.

1965 — Mrs. F. Rachford nursing her eighth baby.

1966 — Mrs. John Welsh nursing one of her twin boys, while cuddling big brother Daniel.

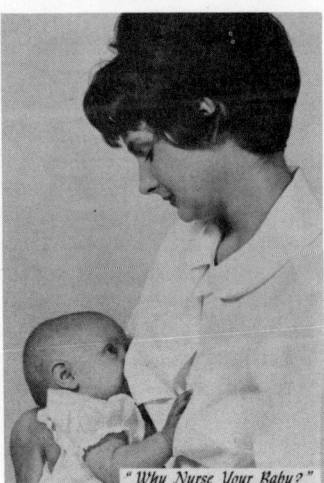
1967 — Mrs. Eugene Filas nursing Catherine, her fourth child.

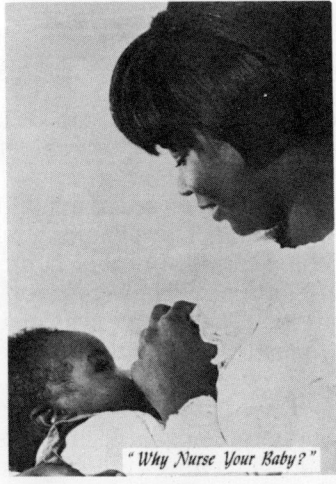
1968 — Harriet J. Murray with Robert, six months old.

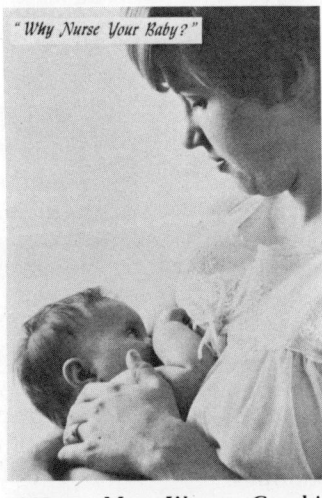
1969 — Mrs. Wayne Gorski (Rita) nursing Kathryn.

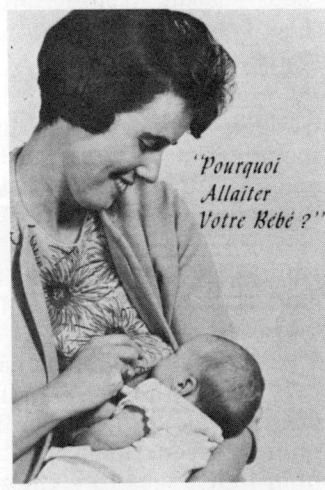
1969 — Mrs. Paul Doucette nursing Marybeth.

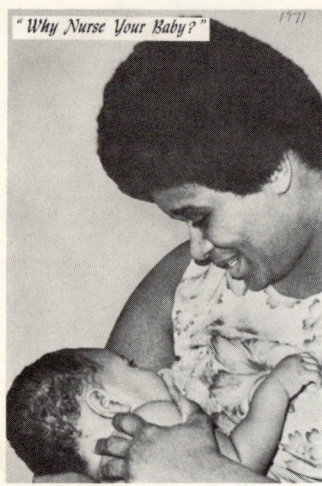
1972 — Mrs. Joseph Hardin (Marsha) nursing Brice.

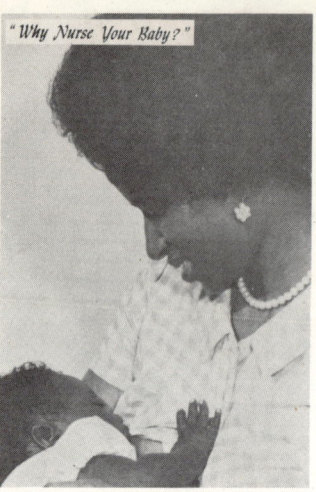
1974 — Margaret Armstrong with Anika Kai, four months old.

1969 — Gilberte Biron nursing Jean-Francois.

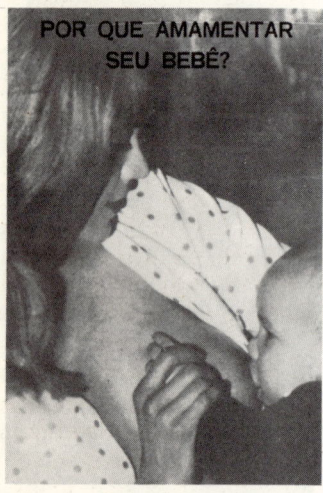
1973 — Emily Rapp nursing Alan Edward.

1976 — Lise Raynauld nursing her baby.

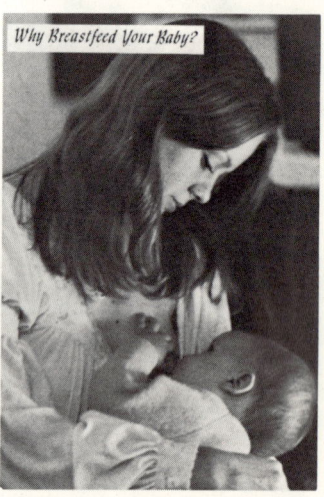
1976 — Denae Leigon nursing Kristan.

paragraph titled, "Mothering is our objective" was included: "Our aim is to help mothers give and enjoy giving happiness and security to their babies through breastfeeding. The unique relationship between mother and her breast-fed infant affords a natural and sure start in good mothering. Much more than the best food for baby, breastfeeding is the best start in living."

A photograph rather than a line drawing was first used with the 1961 edition of the brochure. It featured founding mother Betty Wagner with baby number seven, Helen. The brochure was expanded from four pages to eight and was professionally printed. This was the first time an advertiser, Crib Diaper Service, Inc., used the back cover for advertising and paid for printing the pamphlet.

With minor additions and revisions, the pamphlet has remained essentially the same since 1961. Many mothers and babies have graced the cover over the years.

In 1975 the title of the pamphlet was changed to "Why Breastfeed Your Baby?" The change was made principally for clarification. In other countries, particularly England and New Zealand, 'nurse' means 'take care of.' The change was also made because, at last, 'breastfeeding' had become a socially acceptable word.

The pamphlet is and always has been distributed free of charge. It is designed to acquaint mothers with the advantages of breastfeeding and with the services of La Leche League. Through the brochure, the founding mothers hoped to make mothers everywhere aware of the help that was available if they wanted to nurse their babies.

...Broadens Its Scope

Although he was known only to a very limited number of people in the mid-fifties, all of the founding mothers were well aware of England's Dr. Grantly Dick-Read. His book, *Childbirth Without Fear*, was the only book available on natural childbirth at that time, and all of the founders had used it to enable them to have unmedicated births.

"It was literally a case of having the baby by the book," Edwina recalled.

When Edwina read in the *Natural Childbirth Trust Newsletter* from Great Britain that Dr. Dick-Read was coming to the United States on a speaking tour, she decided at once that Franklin Park should be part of his tour.

He was coming to the United States to speak to various groups of doctors, but Edwina felt there was ample justification for the League's asking him to stop in Franklin Park.

"I'd like to know who better deserves to have Dr. Dick-Read come and talk to them," Edwina reasoned. "After all, we are the mothers who are having the babies his way, so why shouldn't he want to talk to us, too?"

"Our original thought was to have him give a small talk to just a few people," Betty explained.

He was due in the United States in just two months, October of 1957, so the founding mothers quickly sent off a letter with their request. They could hardly believe it when he wrote back and said he would be delighted to come—for $700.00!

"When he said $700.00, I thought that would surely close the issue," Betty recalled. But they decided to try again and sent off another letter explaining that they were a very small group with very limited funds, and wouldn't he please come for less—much less.

Dr. Dick-Read wrote back and assured them that just his name would draw enough people to pay his fee and not to worry.

There were seven very excited women and seven very nervous husbands in Franklin Park in the weeks that followed as the founders made preparations for his visit. They reserved the Franklin Park high school auditorium, sent out news releases, and mailed flyers to a few doctors and medical schools.

"What happened was an incredible thing," Marian recalled. "We didn't have the money or even the addresses to do a big mailing, and the major newspapers refused to print the information we sent them. Only the *Chicago Daily News* printed anything, and it was just one small paragraph. We had absolutely no idea if anybody was going to come.

"Dr. White and I and little Sheila went downtown to pick Dr. Dick-Read up, and when we got back to the auditorium there were buses parked there and people were being turned away. It was amazing!"

People from three states came to hear Dr. Dick-Read. Every one of the 1,250 seats in the Leyden High School auditorium was taken, and hundreds more were turned away. Franklin Park had never seen anything like it before or since!

"It was decided that as president of the League, I would introduce him," Marian said. "One of the husbands in those unliberated days wasn't so sure that a woman should introduce such an important person. But when it was over he told me that I really did well!"

"We pulled the right thing out of the hat at the right time," Mary Ann Cahill said. "There was an interest in this kind of thing, but it had never been focused and pulled together before."

The founding mothers held a reception for Dr. Dick-Read at Mary White's home after his talk. Mary Ann Cahill, who attended the reception with five-day-old Joseph, recalled that it wasn't at all like meeting a celebrity when she met Grantly Dick-Read.

"We were all part of a subculture and we took to each other on that basis," she said. "It was more a case of our all being cohorts together rather than his being a celebrity whom we were privileged to meet."

Excitement ran very high that night. "We provided him with the biggest, most exciting group on his tour," Edwina recalled. "He was tremendously pleased over the large turnout and the interest shown."

There was another dimension to the founding mothers' excitement in addition to having achieved their goal of having Dr. Dick-Read come to Franklin Park. Not only had they covered their expenses in hosting him, but they had made a profit of $350.00. They had been thinking for some time that they really ought to print up some information for mothers who lived too far away to attend meetings. Suddenly, here was the money that would make it possible.

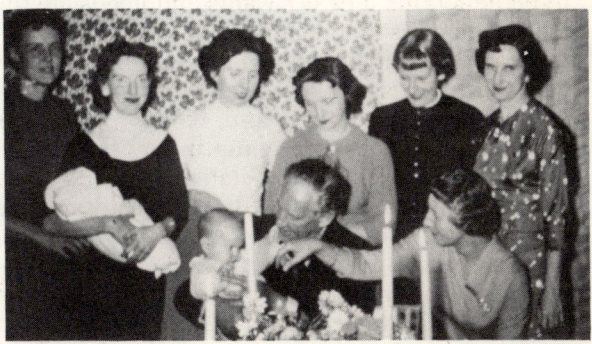

Grantly Dick-Read and his wife Jessica admire Peter Froehlich. Looking on (left to right) are Edwina, Mary Ann Cahill and Joseph, Mary White, Marian, Viola, and Betty.

...Crystallizes Its Goal

In March of 1958, with a year and a half of League meetings behind them, and many happy nursing couples to their credit, Dr. Ratner gathered the founders together to help them clarify the goal of La Leche League.

"We owe our goal to that evening discussion with Dr. Ratner where he tried to broaden our horizons," Mary Ann Kerwin explained. "We were all pretty much ready to zero in on breastfeeding per se, but he felt we should make our goal broader."

"He was trying to get us to realize that we shouldn't put so much emphasis on scientific arguments for breastfeeding," Mary White added. "We were all gung-ho on every latest scientific finding on lower percentage of allergies and all those medical goodies."

"He kept probing and asking questions almost to the point of irritation," Edwina said, "and we were wondering what he was getting at. He kept saying, 'What else is it besides the techniques of breastfeeding that you talk about?' And finally we said, 'Well—mothering!'

"And he said, 'That's it. That's what I wanted you to understand. You really are not talking just about the techniques of breastfeeding, because that is not what is so attractive to the mothers and keeping them coming. It's the fact that you're all together supporting each other in your basic belief that this baby needs good mothering.'"

Mary Ann Cahill later wrote the following account of the meeting for the second issue of the League newsletter, July/August 1958:

Pipe in hand for an emphatic opening gesture, Dr. Herbert Ratner started the discussion. "What is the purpose of La Leche League? How is it being accomplished?"

The League's purpose, Board members agreed, is to help women breastfeed their babies. One of the group explained, "We show mothers how to manage the actual nursing and we talk on the many advantages of nursing to mother and baby. You know, all those impressive statistics on immunities and such."

Our discussion leader knew the statistics, had a high appreciation for them, could add to the list. However, he continued, "La Leche League has an encouraging record of success. What, in the main, accounts for this? Do you believe that learning the mechanics of nursing and listening dutifully to the statistics — necessary as that is — will sustain a nursing mother when she's struggling to calm a fussy baby?"

Questions, as wielded by the good doctor, are delicate but relentless probing testing instruments!

The Board members paused to ponder and shook their collective motherly heads. No, a statistic on immunities or cancer prevention is out the window when the baby is out of sorts. Do the member-mothers give up nursing then? Again, no! A phone call, a visit, making another League meeting, and the troubled mother invariably works things out, ends up talking enthusiastically about her nursing baby. This *talk*, now. The hint it gives of successful nursing as a start to successful mothering!

For between and around and after the words on know-how and statistics at the meetings is the *talk* of the mothers about their nursing experiences. Mothers who have nursed or are nursing (many continue to attend meetings even after completing a series) will recall an "off-day," then quickly reassure another questioning mother that it's no reason to doubt herself or her milk. Or will smilingly admit to well-organized housewife's pangs at having dust on the living room tables after the baby comes. And then the happy realization that shining table tops just don't compete with the joy and peacefulness of nursing one's baby.

Talk that has a constantly recurring theme. The quick, strong love-ties so natural between a nursing mother and her baby. The mother's sure understanding of her baby's needs and her joy and confidence in herself to satisfy them. The happy dividends from this good relationship as the baby grows up. A theme first sensed, gradually understood and absorbed, finally realized by a mother as she nurses her own baby.

A goal for La Leche League, the Board members unanimously concluded. Help mothers successfully breastfeed their babies, and so successfully *mother* them.

...Realizes Baby Knows Best

The belief that a baby's wants and needs are the same is the basis for the philosophy that the founding mothers contributed to La Leche League. Although the 1940s and 50s were a time when babies were strictly scheduled and when a mother's biggest worry was spoiling her infant, the founding mothers ignored the dictates of the day and followed their instincts in filling the baby's needs as completely and totally as possible.

The League's position on baby-led weaning — that ideally the baby should be allowed to continue to nurse for as long as he indicates the need — seems an obvious extension of the founding mothers' philosophy. Yet the founders did not all experience baby-led weanings with their own early babies. They became convinced of the wisdom of baby-led weaning only after years of experience and much soul-searching.

"When we first got together and began talking about breastfeeding, I had already nursed four babies," Betty said. "But still, when you get together and hear other people tell how they managed, you learn even at that stage. That's when we first started questioning weaning. I had weaned all of my children at nine or ten months because everybody said that was when you weaned."

Mary Ann Cahill remembers the prevailing social attitudes about weaning.

"Everybody's mind was tuned to the fact that the *mother* weaned the *baby*. Weaning was something a mother *did*," she explained. Not knowing that there was any alternative to consider, Mary Ann took an active part in weaning her first several children before the end of their first year.

"I had many doubts about my ability to nurse," she said. "I thought I was supposed to wean them, and I didn't think nursing was that much of a need any more. It isn't easy to be the only one doing something, and no one talked about nursing longer."

Mary Ann remembers that the founding mothers were uncertain about the wisdom of late weaning when they first began exploring the idea. "We weren't at all sure ourselves about late weaning. We'd heard that nursing an older baby, particularly a son, could produce undesirable traits. We worried about these things."

Vi Lennon well remembers her pre-League thinking on weaning. She was a patient of Dr. White's, and although she had never met Mary White, she had heard about her.

"I heard through the grapevine that Mary White had nursed a baby for over a year," Vi said. "Everybody told me that you should nurse a baby for nine months. I thought that anybody who nursed a baby for over a year must be weird. I didn't even want to meet her."

Edwina was the first of the founding mothers to nurse a baby for an extended period of time, and she remembers how the other founders watched and waited to see how it would all turn out.

"We were all together when Peter came along (1957), so I had lots of support," Edwina said. "I let him go on as long as he wanted, which was two years and four months. I admit I got a little nervous on and off! We didn't know anybody at that time who had nursed that long. It was a brand new thing."

Betty and Edwina recalled how the founding mothers' thinking on weaning evolved.

"We started giving a lot of thought to weaning and discovered that although the medical textbooks said it should take place no later then nine months, they didn't offer a solid reason why," Betty said. "Some doctors said it was because babies had to learn at an early age how to eat with a fork. Others implied that if a mother didn't forcibly wean, some unprintable disaster might occur in the child's future."

Dr. White and Dr. Ratner admitted they didn't know any good reason why a baby should wean at a particular time.

"It gradually dawned on us," said Edwina, "that we were asking the wrong people. Doctors were men, and why should they know more about it than mothers? Since it wasn't a medical question, their medical education was no help. That was why no good answer could be found in the medical books. We decided that it would be much more likely to be a *woman*, a *mother*, who would know.

"We finally concluded," Edwina said, "that if a baby didn't want to wean, there was no good reason for insisting on it."

"One of the best things that ever happened to me was when I did relax and nurse longer," Mary Ann Cahill said. "There is a very special relationship between the mother and this older baby. I hate to think that mothers don't experience nursing the older baby or enjoy it as fully as they could."

...Writes A Book

When the founding mothers started their little neighborhood group for friends who wanted to nurse their babies, they fully expected it to be just one more of the many organizations they participated in. But it wasn't long before involvement in La Leche League became a major part of their lives.

"It sort of took over our lives," Betty remembered.

"It blotted out everything else," Edwina recalled. "We found that there were no other activities we could be bothered with. We were all the kind of women who were involved in various parish and community activities. But one by one they just got in our way, and we would say, 'No, League is more important. I can't take that on this year.' We had to give all of our time to the League. It took over everything but the care of our children and our husbands."

Although the founding mothers only set out to help their friends who wanted to nurse their babies, word of the help they offered spread quickly beyond the confines of Franklin Park.

"There was a kind of network of people who were interested in the same things," Edwina explained. "We knew Charlotte Aiken, publisher of the *Child-Family Digest*. She had contacts with people all over the country who were interested in an organization like ours.

"The *Child-Family Digest* was a goldmine of wonderful articles on all phases of mothering — childbirth, breastfeeding, child development, and nutrition," Mary White said. "Charlotte Aiken was our guiding light, and the *Digest* was our meat and potatoes. The Aikens supplied the seven of us with large doses of support, and we soaked up everything in the *Digest* like sponges."

"We used to read and reread those copies of the *Child-Family Digest*," Marian recalled. "It supported the way we were inclined and was a good education for us. That magazine had a lot of influence on a lot of people."

"There were women we had helped who had relatives in other towns who wanted help, too," Edwina said. "They would pass along our address, and we began hearing from the relatives. Then some of the women from Franklin Park would move away to other states, and word about the League got spread that way, too."

So, primarily by word of mouth, news about La Leche League began to spread. The organization was little more than a year old when it began averaging fifty or more letters a month and numerous phone calls.

"That was a great number of letters for us to handle because we were all home with little children," Edwina said. "It took a lot of time to answer all those letters, so they piled up very quickly."

"We all did tons of letter writing at home surrounded by our babies and children," Mary Ann Kerwin recalled. "We knew we were repeating the same information and suggestions over and over again."

It was in response to the never-ending stream of mail and the frantic phone calls that the founding mothers decided in 1957 that they needed to put all their information in printed form.

"It was the continual backlog of mail that drove us to getting our information printed up," Edwina explained. "We thought that was going to be the answer to handling all the letters. We thought that if we could get the information written down and sent out, that would gradually cut down on the mail. Of course, that's not the way it worked out. All those letters kept right on coming."

The Grantly Dick-Read lecture gave them a few hundred dollars they could use for printing, and they began thinking about just *what* they should print.

Originally they envisioned a Course By Mail for mothers living too far away to attend meetings. The introduction explained:

When you subscribe to the League, you'll meet another nursing mother who will personally consider your situation. She has the combined experience of all the other mothers of the League to draw on plus access to a great deal of the new material written on the subject in recent years...This mother will mail the Course By Mail, our "Story" of nursing to you in the manner she judges most helpful.

The Course By Mail was chiefly the work of Mary White, Edwina Froehlich, and Mary Ann Cahill, with the others offering suggestions and criticisms as they read it over. After an Introduction telling about La Leche League, it was divided into seven sections: Benefits of Breastfeeding; Planning for Baby; Common Worries; "How-To"; The Father's Role*; Nutrition; and a catch-all final section covering weaning, toilet training, and discipline. Finally, there was a brief description of the seven founding mothers.

The Course was all printed up on forty 8½ x 11 sheets and ready to be mailed out, section by section, when the founders realized that this piecemeal presentation wasn't the best approach.

---

*This section as originally written was largely based on the ideas of a doctor of psychology at the University of Chicago. It didn't seem to quite suit, though, and by the time of the second printing six months later, it had been re-written by a League mother, Dorothy Vining, on the basis of the ideas about fathers expounded by Dr. Ratner. Interestingly, search has so far failed to turn up any copies of that first printing with the Father's Role à la Bruno Bettelheim.

"In the beginning, we didn't think the mothers would want the answer to everything at once," Mary Ann Cahill explained. "Many of them just wrote for answers to a specific problem. We designed the Course By Mail so that we could send each mother whatever parts she wanted, not necessarily the whole thing.

"Then we realized that the mother really needed the whole thing in front of her. She might only be writing about sore nipples, but we began to see that

---

"We thought that if we could get the information written down it would cut down on all that mail. But all those letters kept right on coming."

---

she needed a whole background of information—she needed the whole picture. And we wanted her to get the mothering ideas—not to watch the clock but to respond to the baby."

So the founding mothers simply put it all together in loose-leaf folders from the local variety store and sold the resulting manuals (which still referred to the Course By Mail!) for $2.00 each.

"I couldn't see the need for a book," Vi Lennon said. "I gave everyone a hard time about it. It never occurred to me that people from all over the United States would want it. But all those letters coming in from other states finally changed my mind."

Over the next five years 17,000 copies of the manual were sold — a total of 680,000 pages, hand-collated by the founders and their families and friends to save money.

"But we never mailed a manual without a personal letter," Mary Ann Kerwin said.

The founding mothers knew that helpful and valuable as the manual was, it would never replace the most important thing La Leche offered — mother-to-mother support.

What were the founding mothers like when this first manual was written? They offered these descriptions of each other as a postscript to their motherly advice and ideas in the manual:

Soft-spoken, petite (size 9) MARIAN TOMPSON* manages the presidency of LaLeche and her family of five little girls with the serenity of a Madonna. The one-way blessing of five daughters, no sons, has not discouraged the Tompsons. After baby Sheila's birth they philosophized, "Next time, God willing." The present time was for loving their beautiful new little girl.

Marian's understanding ear and pleasant disposition are exactly the qualities needed to hear and coordinate the variety of ideas of six eager women besides herself — especially when all six of them are popping with suggestions at the same time. Oh, those Board Meetings! Only Marian could do such a smooth job of running them.

* * * * * * * * * * *

*Actually an unfortunate typo here made Marian "Marion." This bothered a lot of people, but Marian herself took it philosophically. She still doesn't complain either about "Marion" or "Thompson" when letter writers miscall her.

24

A completely relaxed manner, time for everybody AND a sense of humor is the perfect foil for a busy life as doctor's wife, mother of seven, author (articles on breast feeding naturally) and "Official Head of Research" for LaLeche. You'll have to ask tall, slim MARY WHITE how to carry it all off well, along with such delightful surprises as a flying trip to Washington, D.C. on a one-day's notice. Of course, the then 6-month old Michael went along, ala papoose, yet! Mike sat grinning from behind his mother's shoulder resting comfortably in a simple little pack-on-the-back which had been advertised in a magazine as mountain climbing equipment. If you live in Franklin Park you might see him now and then in the same spot as his mother whirls around the ice skating rink or whizzes by on her bike.

* * * * * * * * * * * *

Many a blue eye shines, EDWINA FROEHLICH's eyes have a sparkle that almost crackles! When they do, things start to pop —and LaLeche loves it! Articulate, warm-hearted Edwina is the perfect choice for handling correspondence, or for that matter a telephone call for help or an impromptu speech on breast feeding. She also has an article on home delivery to her credit (tells of her own experience) and is the editor of LaLeche's Course By Mail. Three lively sons keep her in shape. (Has naturally curly hair, too! Sigh...)

* * * * * * * * * * * *

The look of a college coed and the shine of a little girl with a new doll belies the fact that MARY ANN KERWIN is the mother of two boys and an exceptionally conscientious librarian for LaLeche League. Her job includes reading (which Mary Ann says she does while nursing) and cataloging (which she most likely does after baby is in bed) a so-o-o high stack of periodicals on breastfeeding and related subjects. Mary Ann has a special appeal to young girls, has given talks on breast feeding and natural childbirth to several such groups.

* * * * * * * * * * * *

Blessed with an uncommonly good share of good common sense, BETTY WAGNER can be counted on to keep things — such as LaLeche League — on an even keel. No impractical nonsense is passed with Betty on the job! Her official capacity is Treasurer, and she cheerfully accepts any and all donations to LaLeche, at times nags the Board about unpaid printer's or book bills. In her unofficial capacity at meetings as Baby Soother, First Class, she really excels and is certainly appreciated!

Betty has five children, gracefully passes off remarks of "Such a young mother. Can this young lady be your daughter?" when seen with her oldest, fifteen-year old Gail.

* * * * * * * * * * * *

Smart, and smart-looking VIOLA LENNON could have stepped out of a page of any fashion magazine, would be a sensation as *the* New Look — a nursing mother! Viola's busy schedule and distance from the groups now limits her participation in LaLeche affairs to an occasional, but bound to be lively, meeting. A good part of that busy schedule are her four youngsters, three daughters and a son, all under the age of six.

* * * * * * * * * * * *

Mother of six assorted-size children, red-haired and chic MARY ANN CAHILL not only looks the part of the lovely young mother but lives the part very well indeed. It is often said that the man is the head of the home and the woman is the heart. Mary Ann's heart reaches beyond her home and her womanly qualities enable her always in our discussions to get straight at the *heart* of the matter; taking us beyond mere words to warm, human understanding. We bet if the LaLeche Board Mothers were to take a vote — Mary Ann Cahill would be chosen as the mother they would least like to do without.

...Issues A Newsletter

The first issue of LA LECHE LEAGUE NEWS appeared in May of 1958. Marian Tompson was its first editor.

"It occurred to me that mothers who were at a distance had no way of knowing the experiences of other mothers or keeping in touch with the latest things going on, so I thought it was important to have a newsletter," Marian explained. "So while the others were starting to put the first manual together, I concentrated on putting out the first newsletter. So naive was I that I didn't even date the first issue!

"It was really to keep mothers in touch and give them somebody else to relate to or identify with or to learn from, because at that time few mothers had anyone in their circle of friends who was breastfeeding," Marian said.

It was decided to issue the newsletter bimonthly, and the subscription price was set at $1.00 per year.

"We printed a hundred copies of the first issue and sent it out free and then asked people if they would like to subscribe. Mary White came over to help me fold and staple them, and I had my daughter Debbie licking the stamps. I remember how she grumbled because she wanted to be outside playing!"

That first issue was five mimeographed pages long and contained a brief history of the League, its founders, its groups and activities. Birth announcements, book reviews, poetry, nutrition tips, and a sampling of League correspondence filled the first pages of the *NEWS*.

Putting out the *NEWS* became a family affair for the Tompsons.

"While I was editor, I wrote the *NEWS* at my dining room table, would get it mimeographed, and then the children would sit around the table and fold them and put stamps on them and send them out."

Though the children were expected to help with the *NEWS*, they could always be confident that they were the first priority in their mother's life. The *NEWS* was late more than once because Marian always put her job as wife and mother first.

In the second issue of the *NEWS* she explained, "We regret that this issue of the *NEWS* is reaching you a few weeks late. But a siege of the regular measles at our house — with five children succumbing at one time — topped off with father's case of blood poisoning, naturally got first priority."

The first two issues were titled *LA LECHE LEAGUE NEWSLETTER*. With the third issue the title was changed to *LA LECHE LEAGUE NEWS*, and the slogan "Mothering thru breastfeeding" was added.

One of the first major issues to be tackled in the *NEWS* was weaning. In the January/February, 1959, *NEWS*, Edwina began a series of articles on weaning. Her first article later was issued as a reprint, "Thoughts about Weaning." In it she suggested letting the baby decide when it was time to wean, rather than arbitrarily weaning him at a certain age. In later issues she described her weaning experiences with her three sons (Paul at nineteen months, David at fourteen months, and Peter at twenty-one months and still nursing at the time of the final article).

"It turned out to be a good thing because I began hearing from a lot of other 'closet nursers.'"

Responses to those articles ranged from a doctor's wife who felt that nursing a toddler would be "but stringing the emotionally immature child along," to the head of the Maternity Institute in New Mexico, who wrote, "It is so thrilling to have mothers themselves taking the initiative in presenting these very sensitive views, and when they do it no one can accuse them of being out of their field."

"I remember I was so excited about those articles when Edwina was writing them," Marian said. "I felt they were such important breakthroughs. As I was typing them up for the *NEWS* I felt they were so important because I had never seen it down in print before. This was the first real exploration and discussion of the issue from the mother's and the baby's viewpoint. I felt it was very exciting and very important. You couldn't find that information any place else in the United States at that time.

"I remember the first time I talked about nursing a two-year-old in 'Memos from Marian' (November/December, 1962)," Marian recalled. "I did it with much trepidation because at the time I wrote it I was thinking, 'Maybe some of my relatives will be reading this and they don't know that Brian is two years old and still nursing.' But it turned out to be a good thing because as a result of writing it I began hearing from other 'closet nursers' who said, 'I'm still nursing my baby and nobody knows it.'"*

In 1959 LaVerne Bollig, an early and enthusiastic member of the League, took over the job of circula-

*Apparently it's still a ticklish subject. Mary Carson, now editor of the *LLL NEWS*, says that almost every time she prints an article mentioning nursing older babies or toddlers, she gets some indignant flak about it—not nearly as much as formerly, though, and there are many more letters like the one that said (May, 1977), "Bless you for putting in the article of the lady who nursed her three-year-old. I'm still nursing my 14-month-old son with a lot of upraised eyebrows from my Gyn. Dr. and friends. This is #2 son, and my hubby is more understanding this time around (my first I only nursed for 11 months—too many were against me and I gave up the fight).
...Thank you for all your encouragement and all the ladies who have helped me around the country when we were "on the move"—Richmond, Va., Houston, Tex., and now here in Harrisburg, Pa."

tion manager of the *NEWS*, and a year later Mary Ann Cahill became editor. Mary Ann remembers how strongly she felt about the moral support and information that the *NEWS* was providing.

"The mothers needed constant reinforcement," she said. "They had to know that nursing their babies was worthwhile. Now it's more commonly recognized that breastfeeding is the best way to feed a baby, but in those days people thought the scientists had come up with something pretty good with bottles. Bottles were the new and improved way. The mothers needed to be constantly encouraged and to hear about other mothers who thought that nursing a baby was worthwhile."

Those early issues of the *NEWS* were mimeographed on 8½×14 inch paper.

Toward the end of 1960, Meredith and Floyd Arnold of Lunenburg, Vermont, travelled to Franklin Park with an interesting suggestion. They and their son, Matthew, were just home from Stuttgart, Germany, where Floyd had been studying printing on a Fulbright scholarship. A copy of *THE WOMANLY ART* had gone with them, and baby Matthew, born in Germany, had the benefit of it.

Floyd and his artist wife felt that the newsletter of an organization as important as La Leche League should be more attractive and professional in appearance. The Arnolds offered their services, and for the next year and a half the *NEWS* was printed at their press in Vermont and sent to Franklin Park to be mailed out. An unwieldy arrangement; but the Arnolds' talents turned the *NEWS* into an attractive ten-page 7x8½ inch publication, of which editor Mary Ann Cahill wrote in its first issue (March, 1961):

> Who says a newsletter can't strut, once it's done up in such a grand fashion. Floyd and Meredith Arnold of Lunenburg, Vermont, who are responsible for the new look of *LA LECHE LEAGUE NEWS*, claim the paper was no sooner off their presses than it positively puffed like a peacock.
> We haven't heard from the post office yet, but we wouldn't be a bit surprised to hear it pranced through second class mail, quite the envy of all the other Newsletters.

The founding mothers took advantage of the colorful redesigned nameplate to improve on the slogan it carried, which became "Good Mothering Through Breastfeeding."

In format and appearance, the *NEWS* still reflects the Arnolds' influence.

When Marybeth Doucette took over as circulation manager with the May/June, 1961, issue, the subscription list of the *NEWS* had swelled to an astronomical total of about six hundred names. The problems of the long-distance printing arrangement became too great, and with the November/December, 1962, issue, John Hudetz (husband of Gwen Hudetz, leader of the LLL group in Warrenville, Illinois) began printing the *NEWS*. At the same time, Mary Ann Kerwin's sister, Florence Carlson, also of Warrenville, became the editor, with Lea Murphy as associate editor. And the *NEWS* went sailing along.

...Becomes Incorporated

It was in September of 1958 that La Leche League filed with the State of Illinois and became La Leche League of Franklin Park, Inc.

"We did it to please our husbands," Betty explained. "If your organization is not incorporated you are personally liable for any debts the group incurs. If you are incorporated, only the group is liable."

There were seven husbands who didn't sleep well as the Dick-Read lecture money was used up and the bills from the printer for the manual and reprints started climbing toward $1,000. Incorporating was the logical solution.

"Incorporation also gave us tax-free status in Illinois," Betty said. "And a real sense of permanence."

...Formalizes Its Organization

The founding mothers quickly got into the habit of meeting regularly to handle group business and pool their ideas on interesting or unusual nursing situations. These meetings became known as board meetings.

"We realized that somebody had to be responsible for the organization," Edwina explained. "No matter how big or how little it was, you had to have people responsible for running it. So the seven of us said, 'We're like a board.'"

As mothers in the League groups expressed interest in deeper involvement with the League, they, too, were invited to these meetings.

"When we started out, anyone who was leading a group was invited to the board meetings," Edwina explained. "What we would get together to discuss was primarily the content of the meetings. In those days, it was the mothering things we were concerned with. We weren't talking about organizational matters and such. We needed to learn how to advise all of those mothers who were used to giving bottles and whose doctors were telling them they had to give bottles. We talked about the best way to present our position on starting solids. We were bucking the whole medical establishment when we recommended late solids. These were the problems we dealt with at the board meetings."

During the late 1950s and early 60s the board meetings became very popular and grew in both size and scope.

> **"They knew Mary White had a good size family and was a doctor's wife, and they valued her suggestions especially."**

"A lot of women came to talk over mothering questions, problems they were having with different age children," Edwina explained. "They knew Mary White had a good size family and was a doctor's wife, and they valued her suggestions especially."

Other women were attracted to the board meetings by the variety and depth of information that was available there.

"We shared with the mothers at the board meetings things that we didn't talk about at regular meetings — a controversial article on breastfeeding, new research, an in-depth discussion of our mothering philosophy," Edwina said. "The mothers were hungry for this kind of information

> **"In those days, it was the mothering things we were concerned with."**

and the board meetings provided a place where they could share and learn from each other."

The meetings quickly became so large that they had to be held in an assembly room at the Franklin Park Police Station to accommodate the crowds.

"All of the women who were starting groups would come, and sometimes they would bring other mothers with them who were active in their groups," Edwina said. "We really hadn't gotten around to much structure then. We were just concerned about what was being said in the groups and getting the latest information to the leaders."

By the early 1960s, fifty to sixty women were attending the bimonthly board meetings. The founding mothers began to feel that the size of the group was interfering with the effectiveness of the meetings.

"By this time we were spending more and more of our time on business and felt we should be covering more in the way of philosophy," Betty explained. "It was impossible to accomplish much of anything with a group that size."

Late in 1962 the decision was made to split the board meetings into several smaller sections. The divisions were made geographically, and the smaller local sections became known as chapters. There were approximately five groups in each chapter. The smaller size and more local nature of the chapters made it possible for leaders to share ideas on situations they were encountering in their groups and to have in-depth discussions of League philosophy.

Because the local chapters had their own boards, the founding mothers then became known as the Executive Board. It became the function of the Executive Board to pass policies affecting both the content of the meetings and the organizational structure.

Far from the former size of fifty or more, the Executive Board consisted of the seven founding mothers and several women they asked to serve on the Board with them. The Executive Board continued to meet as often as needs determined to make policies and administer the organizational aspects of the ever-growing La Leche League.

...Expands Its Lines Of Communication

Mothers wanting breastfeeding help from the League would either call or write, depending on their distance and the urgency of their situation. Since she was Executive Secretary, Edwina's home address was used as the League's official address. It was also Edwina's phone number that was given as the number to call for breastfeeding help.

"I was the logical one to handle the calls because I had the smallest family," Edwina said. "I only had the three boys, and they were at an age where I felt I could handle the phone calls."

For several years the Froehlich family's personal phone number was given out as La Leche League's number. But by 1959 two factors spurred the founders to put a separate line into Edwina's home for League calls.

Edwina and Peter — "Sometimes I had to go count the egg shells in the garbage."

"We wanted to be listed as La Leche League in the telephone book," Edwina said. "A lot of people were being frustrated because they had heard of us but couldn't find a telephone listing for us. They knew the name La Leche League, but they didn't know our individual names."

The second reason the founders obtained a separate number for the League was because they felt there was a need to separate personal calls from League calls.

"Many of us had husbands who were having a hard time getting through to us during the day!" Edwina said.

A separate number for League calls also made it possible for Edwina not to answer that phone at times when her family needed her attention.

> *"A lot of people were frustrated because they had heard of us but couldn't find a telephone listing for us."*

"I didn't want to not answer my own phone because it might be someone in the family with an urgency that I needed to respond to," she explained. "But with the League phone it was possible not to answer it when I was putting dinner on the table or when the boys needed my attention.

"I had a long cord on the phone that would reach from the front porch to the back yard," she said. "I could be on the phone and still walk to wherever I needed to be at the moment."

Edwina recalled that she quickly learned to do household tasks while talking on the telephone.

"But it could get confusing," she said, "particularly when I was cooking. Sometimes I had to go count the egg shells in the garbage!"

In the beginning, Edwina received both local and long distance phone calls on the League phone. But by the time she gave up the League phone in 1964 she was getting primarily long distance calls.

"As the League grew, there were more and more people to call who were able to help mothers, and most of the local calls were diverted to the groups," she said. "I was getting mostly long distance calls from total strangers who didn't know anyone in League but had gotten the phone number from somewhere."

Edwina passed on the League phone in 1964 when it became necessary for her to spend more of her time on other pressing League matters.

...Loses A Founder To Denver

In 1960 Tom and Mary Ann Kerwin decided to move to Denver, Colorado.

"When we moved to Denver I found it very difficult to leave my La Leche League friends," Mary Ann said. "They had become an integral part of my life.

"During the eight months we were planning the move, I handled all of the League correspondence from mothers living in Colorado so that I would know the people there. I was six months pregnant when we moved, so I figured the best thing to do was start LLL of Colorado right away before I had a new little baby.

"I called all of the contacts I had made through letter writing and set up a meeting for February, 1960. It was one of the first League groups outside the Chicago area.

"I was dreading the unknown as far as childbirth

The Kerwins exploring their new home state — Eddie, Greg, Mary Ann, Tommy, 1960.

in Denver was concerned, but Dr. White assured me I couldn't move to a better place in the world for natural childbirth because Dr. Robert Bradley was there. He was one of the foremost proponents at that time of true natural childbirth and had physical therapists teaching pregnant women natural childbirth exercises.

"When I went for my first office visit with Dr. Bradley and told him I was one of those who had assisted in starting La Leche League, he said, 'We welcome you with open arms.' And he did. Immediately, he wanted brochures on LLL of Colorado and gave one to each of his patients. He did and does give 100% support to breastfeeding as well as to natural childbirth. He told all of his patients to go to those nursing mothers' meetings.

"I quickly chose my first co-leader, Anne Theobald. Another early leader was Rhondda Hartman, one of Dr. Bradley's exercise teachers, who helped me improve on my natural childbirth while I helped her with breastfeeding. She actually began labor at one of our early League meetings,

> ***"Often we found mother's milk turned heartache to joy, but the vast majority of our help involved simply encouraging mothers to happily breastfeed their babies."***

leaving from our house for a happy delivery.

"We were also fortunate to have strong medical support from the start from outstanding doctors such as Dr. L. Joseph Butterfield of the Children's Hospital, who started the Newborn Center there and introduced the idea of 'mothering-in' for premature infants in the 1960s. He was most helpful as an advisor, and now is on the LLLI Professional Advisory Board. He did all he could to help us be accepted by the medical community.

"Dr. Fritz Mijer, a pediatrician with a 99% breastfed practice and a member of the LLLI Professional Advisory Board, was also most helpful as an advisor to us, helping with many of our crisis cases.

"We organized one of the first LLL chapters outside the Chicago area. I was president for about five years, and we had monthly chapter meetings in my home with typically numerous babies and toddlers. This Colorado chapter was the foundation for La Leche League of Colorado, Wyoming, and Montana.

"When we started out I asked diaper services to publish our brochures in return for one or two line

> ***"Dr. White assured me I couldn't move to a better place in the world for natural childbirth."***

ads and begged for publicity from our local newspapers. Finally in 1961 we had a long article written on LLL of Colorado in the Sunday magazine section of the *Denver Post*. Now publicity is much easier to come by, and we have been featured on numerous television shows as well as in the newspapers.

"Often we found mother's milk turned heartache to joy," Mary Ann said, "but the vast majority of our help involved simply encouraging mothers to happily breastfeed their babies."

...Hires Its First Employee

By the spring of 1963, La Leche League and Edwina Froehlich had reached a crisis.

"I was completely overwhelmed by all the mail," Edwina recalled. "I worried about the information the mothers were waiting for that I just wasn't getting to."

The mail had long been more than one person could possibly handle, so Edwina had devised a system whereby she kept the largest share for herself, as secretary, and divided the rest among the other founding mothers. Every morning when the mail came she divided it up, put the others' letters into large manila envelopes, and mailed it on to them.

"It took me an hour or more a day just to open all the mail, sort it, and put it in manila envelopes for the others," Edwina said.

But she was still always behind, and the stack of unanswered letters was constantly growing. She always opened all the letters as soon as they came and answered the emergencies right away. But the pile of nonemergency letters grew and grew and grew.

"Many of them *were* emergencies by the time they got answered," Edwina said. "I finally took the bull by the horns and called up an employment office here in Franklin Park. It was one of those things where I couldn't take it any more—I had to do it."

She told the agency that she needed a stenographer who could work three mornings a week in her home. She insisted on mornings only because her boys came home from school for lunch and she wanted the dining room to be back to normal and the stenographer gone before they got home.

The agency called back ten minutes later and said they had a woman they were sending over.

"I was scared stiff," Edwina recalled, "because I knew that somehow we were going to have to pay for her. But it was the best thing I ever did. I can remember to this day the feeling I had when I got rid of the last letter in the pile and could see the top of my desk again."

The mornings-only arrangement was perfect for the stenographer, too, who also had young sons. So after the backlog of mail had been cleared up she agreed to stay on for a while and help Edwina keep up with the mail.

So far, LaVerne Spadaro's job has lasted fourteen years and still counting.

...Rents Its First Office

The first La Leche League office, other than assorted bedrooms, dining rooms, basements, and garages, came into being in March of 1963. It was born of a growing crisis and was delivered with the help of a doctor—Edwina's podiatrist.

Since the first days of the League, Edwina's dining room had functioned as the League's office, and the bulk of the League's books, reprints, and files were stored in her spare bedroom. The bedroom wasn't much bigger than a large closet, and the filing cabinets and boxes of books stacked to the ceiling completely filled it.

"It hadn't mattered because we weren't using the bedroom," Edwina recalled. But now her oldest son, Paul, needed that bedroom.

"He was no longer happy in the same bedroom with his two younger brothers," she said. "He had outgrown them. He now looked upon the things they had formerly enjoyed doing together as 'kid stuff.' The two younger ones were always in his way. I knew he really should be separated from them and put into that back bedroom. We just had to clear the things out of that bedroom so Paul could have it. But where would we put all that stuff?

"Then one day I was having a corn dug out of the sole of my foot by a podiatrist in town. We got to talking, so naturally I got to telling him about our League."

Edwina explained that she really had a problem because she needed that bedroom for her son, but there was no place to put all the League's things.

"He said to me, 'What you really need is a little office.' And I said, 'Yes, that's just what we need.'

"He asked if we could pay for it, and I said we had a little money but we couldn't afford much. Then he told me there was a small office right

> *"The owner agreed to the $50.00 and no lease, but the battle wasn't quite won."*

down the hall that he was sure we could get because it was just standing vacant. I asked what kind of rent the man was asking and he said, $75.00, but he was sure we could get it for less. The owner was right on the premises and showed me the office right away."

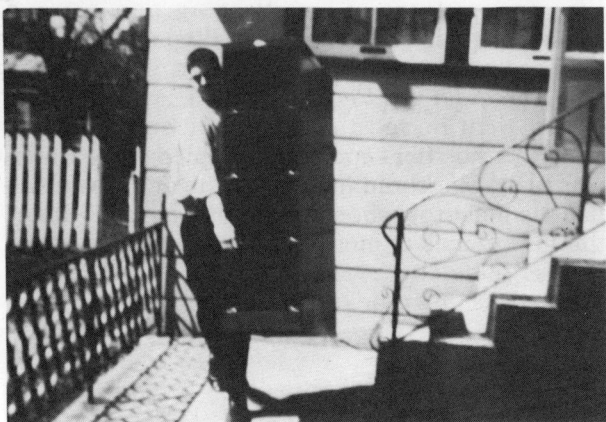
The League files, at long last leaving Paul's bedroom.

Joe and Bill White unloading the car at the new office.

It was just a small one room office, but it was only two blocks from Edwina's home, and Edwina saw that it was the answer to her problem. She told the owner that League didn't have enough money to sign a lease, but she thought they could handle $50.00 a month for a while. The owner agreed to the $50.00 and no lease. But the battle wasn't quite won.

"I rushed right home and called Marian. I told her about this wonderful office I had found. Marian was always very conservative about money so she said, 'Oh, it's just a great idea, but where are we going to get the money?'"

Edwina hung up, wondering why she had been so foolish as to call the most conservative member of the group! But she was determined to have that bedroom for Paul, so she called Betty next.

"Betty had always said we could do whatever we had to do. So she told me, 'If we have to do it, we have to do it. Just go back and tell him you'll take it.'"

Edwina quickly finalized the deal. La Leche League now had a home of its own at 9606 Franklin Avenue. Edwina's father-in-law donated his old desk and chair and coatrack; and Mary White's two oldest boys (who are now doctors) helped Edwina and LaVerne move the things from Edwina's house to the new office.

Paul had his bedroom, Edwina had peace of mind, and La Leche League had its first real home.

...Receives Public Recognition

La Leche League never sought publicity in the early years, but publicity had a way of finding the League.

It never occurred to them to seek publicity, Edwina explained. The founding mothers had more than they could handle in trying to keep up with the demands of their young families and taking care of the mothers they already knew who wanted help. It never crossed their minds to publicize their services.

But it occurred to other people. In 1958 Robert Brizzolara, whose wife was a League leader, brought La Leche League its first publicity. He was a contributing writer for *Marriage*, a magazine with a small Midwest circulation read by young Catholic families. It carried a list of helping organizations, and this husband sent in League's name and address and said they offered help to breastfeeding mothers.

"It was just a little three-line squib stuck someplace between 'financial help' and 'family counseling.'" Edwina remembered. But it brought in about a hundred responses.

"We just couldn't believe it," Edwina recalled. The founding mothers had been too busy with the day-to-day demands of their lives to give any thought to mothers outside of Franklin Park who might want help nursing their babies. The response from *Marriage* was only the first of many deluges of mail in response to publicity about the League.

Beginning in 1958, magazines such as *Baby Talk, Prevention, Herald of Health,* several Catholic publications, a few medical journals, and Chicago newspapers began spreading word of League's work. Articles about La Leche League were in print someplace often enough that from 1958 on there was always a steady stream of outside mail. By 1960, after being in existence for only four years, the League was averaging three hundred phone calls and four hundred letters a month.

The first major national publicity came in May of 1960 from a feature in *Family Circle*. Again, it was the husband of a woman who was attending

League meetings, Richard Frisbie, who submitted the article. It featured a large, tasteful picture of a mother lying in bed nursing her baby, and the large type beside the picture proclaimed, "La Leche League, an astonishing group of women, is determined that nursing—that age-old form of mothering—shall not become a lost art." The feature described at length how and why the League came into existence, what kind of help it offered, and how to get in touch with it for information.

Hundreds and hundreds of requests for help poured into Franklin Park in the following weeks. In the month of May alone, eight hundred letters were delivered to Edwina's home, then the League's official address. By the end of the month, Edwina's weary mailman was suggesting that she open her own post office.

The granddaddy of them all in terms of mail generated was the article by Karen Pryor printed in the May, 1963, *Reader's Digest*.

"The first contact we had with Karen Pryor was in 1960 when I had the League phone in my house," Edwina recalled. "She called and said she was writing a book on breastfeeding and wanted to know if she could look at our files and letters. She said, 'I hope you won't think of me as competition. I am doing an entirely different kind of book than yours.'

"The seven of us had decided long ago that we would work together with anyone who wanted our help and that we would encourage anyone to publish any information they had on breastfeeding. So I told her we would be glad to help her any way we could."

Karen Pryor went to Franklin Park and spent some time at Edwina's house looking through her files and pictures of breastfeeding mothers and talking to some of the other founding mothers.

"She traveled with her children and brought along an older girl to care for them," Edwina said. "They went on most of her interviews with her, and the babysitter kept them occupied while Karen was busy. She could have left them at home if she had wanted to but she shared our philosophy about the importance of mothers and children being together."

When Karen Pryor's book was published in 1963,

Marian and Karen Pryor renewing their friendship at the 1971 convention.

the cover photograph featured Marian with her infant son, Brian.

Reader's Digest excerpted from that book the chapter about La Leche League. Titled, "They Teach the Joys of Breastfeeding," the article gave League its first international publicity when it was printed in the *Digest's* English, Spanish, and French editions. That article brought in thousands and thousands of letters. Karen Pryor graciously donated to the League the $300.00 *Reader's Digest* paid her.

"There has never been anything like the response to that article again," Edwina said, "and we don't expect that there ever will be." For the midsixties brought something of a turning point in breastfeeding in America. Until that time, little published information had been available about it, and when something was printed, the response was tremendous. But after that point, more and more became available about breastfeeding, and anyone wanting information could find it with little trouble.

In less than ten years, breastfeeding had gone from being a nearly lost art to a well-publicized and much talked about style of mothering. The tide had been turned, a trend had been reversed. La Leche League had much of which to be proud.

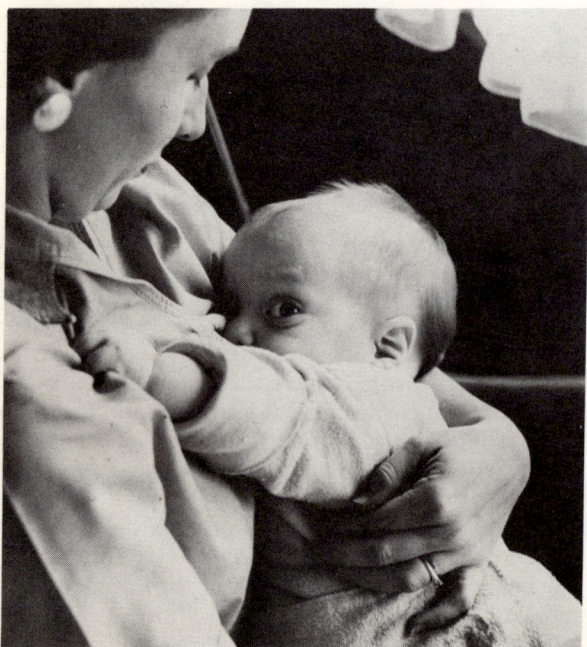

The cover photo from Karen Pryor's NURSING YOUR BABY, featuring Marian Tompson and Brian.

LLLI Founding Mothers, July, 1967 — Mary White with Molly, Marian, Mary Ann Cahill, Edwina, Vi with Gina, Mary Ann Kerwin, and Betty.

Growing Up

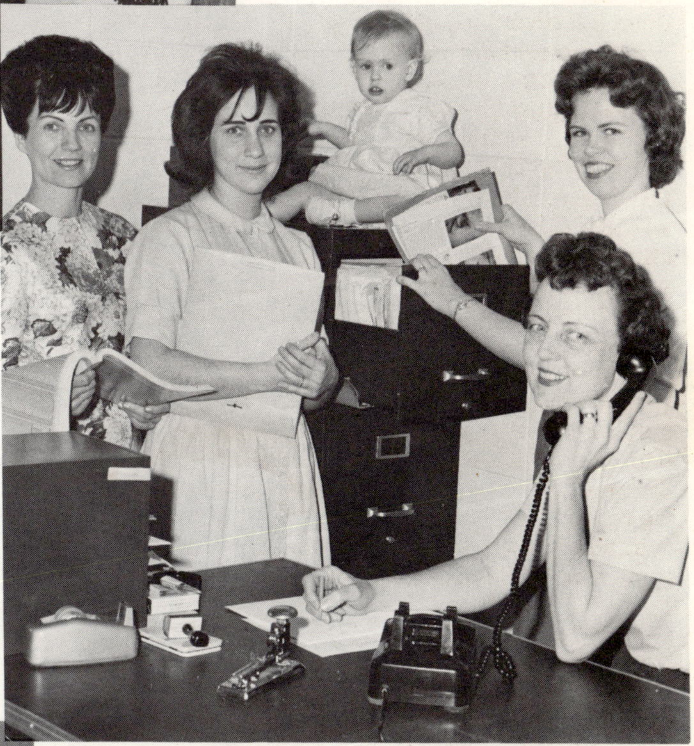

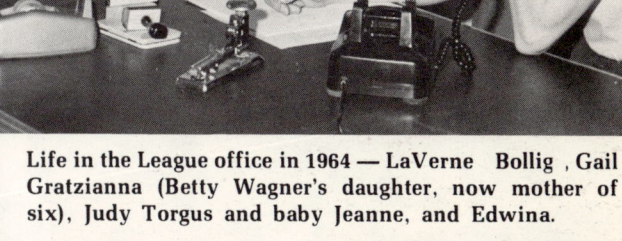

Life in the League office in 1964 — LaVerne Bollig, Gail Gratzianna (Betty Wagner's daughter, now mother of six), Judy Torgus and baby Jeanne, and Edwina.

Marybeth Doucette with Leona, and Judy Torgus with Paul, at 1969 Ohio state meeting.

Edwina and Betty in front of LLLI office, 1971.

33

Writing a "Real" Book

The first manual was hardly back from the printers before the founding mothers realized that they were going to have to revise and expand it.

"It wasn't complete enough," Betty explained. "As soon as it was out we started getting letters about problems and situations that we hadn't covered. We were learning more all the time, and we knew that we would have to write another manual that would include all of the things that we hadn't put in the first one."

Meanwhile, they began writing, and printing in the NEWS, articles on some of the things that weren't in THE WOMANLY ART, or that hadn't been sufficiently covered there. Introducing solids, sore nipples, weight gain... "These were the problems mothers would write about and these were the long distance phone calls we would get," Edwina explained. "So these were the things we tried to get into print right away."

Then it occurred to the founders to reprint these articles so that they could be sent out individually, and La Leche League's series of information sheets was off to a flying start.

"We needed to have something to tuck in an envelope and send to the mother right away when she needed help," Edwina said. "It was too expensive to send the manual first class, so reprints seemed to be the answer."

Then the founding mothers turned their attention to the revision of THE WOMANLY ART. They agreed to switch from the loose-leaf format to a permanently bound edition. They also felt they would like it to be a more polished version than the first one had been—"a regular book"—with illustrations and all the trimmings. But the founders were all mothers of little ones and had neither the time nor the technical knowledge to accomplish this.

> **"Our meetings were frequently canceled because this one had the chicken pox or that one had the mumps."**

As it nearly always seemed to happen, when they needed someone with special talents, someone turned up. It was about this time that Gordon and Mary Carson, community-minded Franklin Parkers, had persuaded Dr. White to write a book about emergency childbirth. Gordon had pointed out to him that the standard first-aid manuals did not cover this situation, and that policemen, cab drivers, and others often called upon to help a woman in childbirth needed to be better informed about the kind of help they could safely give. Dr. White taped the text; Mary Carson, an experienced editor, did the typing and editing; and Gordon published the book (which quickly became, and remains, the standard manual on the subject).

So when the founding mothers began to fret over getting the rewrite of THE WOMANLY ART into proper shape, Dr. White suggested that they ask Mary Carson to help them. Mary had breastfed both her children, though by that time they were both in school.

> **"She was the little elf who took it home every night and put together all the work we'd done."**

Mary agreed at once to lend her expertise.

"From the beginning she was involved in writing the manual," Marian said. "She outlined the chapters, gave us an idea of where the book should be going, and provided us with an organizational structure for the book. She also indexed it, which is a special art. The seven of us could never have done it. The book would not have gotten done without Mary. She was the little elf who took it home every night and put together all the work we'd done."

Even with this help, producing a book was a mammoth undertaking for seven young mothers.

"We had no idea what we were getting into," Mary White recalled. "We decided that this was what we wanted to do, and we just plunged in. It was our enthusiasm that carried us through. We had wonderful times together doing it."

"We often got together at night to write," Mary Ann Kerwin said, "because of our many daytime distractions and the interruptions necessarily built into our roles as mothers. We worked over words like groups of lawyers struggling to clarify a legal brief. Expressing what we wanted to say in the best possible way was our biggest challenge."

"Our meetings were frequently canceled because this one had the chicken pox or that one had the mumps," Edwina recalled. "It was just lucky that most of us lived close enough that we could talk on the phone without its being a toll call."

Edwina remembers the reactions they got from people who heard what they were planning to do.

"Several people at the time said to us, 'Seven people can't write a book. You just can't do that.' And we said, 'Well, maybe no other seven can do it but this seven has got to!'"

"We had to do it," Betty explained, "because by this time we had had national publicity and we had to offer something more than a little loose leaf manual and a few reprints."

"Each of us agreed to work on a different part," Betty explained. "Then as one person finished a section, each of the others would read it and rewrite and add things; then the whole section would get rewritten again. It took a lot of revisions!"

"Whatever someone wrote was bound to be changed," Marian said.

"Then we had to get Dr. White and Dr. Ratner to read it for accuracy," Betty said. "That was like pulling teeth! Viola had the job of getting it out of their hands, and sometimes she would call them three times a day to get them to read it. But it certainly paid off, because they put in a lot of things that we would have never thought of. Their contributions were really great."

"Dr. Ratner kept us from going off on the wrong track," Edwina said. "Places where we would want

> **"Mary White always had the strongest mind and the strongest voice on mothering. We could always agree with what Mary had to say about mothering."**

to be almost militant, he would counsel temperance as a better way. There were times when we would want to come out with a strong statement about something that we felt was absolutely sure. He would say to us, 'Well I certainly tend to agree with you, but you know we don't have any proof, so we can't make an absolute statement like that.' He tempered us. We realized that once you put it into print it's there for everyone to read and reread for many years to come, and if it's not accurate it's pretty sad. He trained us to separate our feelings from actual fact."

The basic principles of good nutrition in the new "Nutritional Know-How" chapter were reprinted almost verbatim from a monograph of Dr. Ratner's. He also contributed a Foreword for the revised manual, in his own inimitable scholarly style.

The line drawings for the revised WOMANLY ART were the work of artist Joy Sidor, who had become involved in La Leche League through her mother.

"I was giving a talk on breastfeeding," Marian recalled, "and afterward a lady came up to me and said that her daughter, Joy, had had a terrible time trying to breastfeed her baby. Joy was due again soon, and her mother wondered if I would help her. A couple of weeks later the baby was born, and Joy's mother called from her bedside and said, 'Now you help her.'"

Marian did; and Joy's gratitude for her happy nursing experience flowered into the charming drawings in THE WOMANLY ART. She has kept in loving touch with Marian and the League, and has contributed the drawings in this book.

> **"Each of us agreed to work on a different part, then the others would read it and rewrite and add things."**

All the founding mothers participated in writing the manual, but the principal writers were Mary White, Mary Ann Cahill, Marian, and Edwina.

"When we were writing the captions for the drawings," Marian said, "I was pregnant and very nauseated. I remember sitting there with Mary Carson at the dining-room table feeling so sick and trying to think up clever captions."

When the revised manual was completed, Marian and Mary Carson pulled it all together and saw it through the press — the press being Interstate Printers and Publishers of Danville, Illinois, which had been recommended to Mary by friends in the publishing field. Hans Paulsen of Interstate helped with the details, becoming "sold" on both the League and breastfeeding in the process, and adding another to the long list of friendly advisors without whom the founding mothers could not have accomplished all they have.

With the book at last at the printer's, the founding mothers heaved a collective sigh of relief.

"The interesting thing in retrospect is our total philosophical agreement," Mary Ann Kerwin said.

> **"Joy's gratitude for her happy nursing experience flowered into the charming drawings in THE WOMANLY ART."**

"It seems amazing," Betty said, "but we didn't ever fight. I don't remember anyone ever being angry. It was the strongest mind that won."

"So much of it was on mothering," Edwina said, "and Mary White always had the strongest mind and the strongest voice on mothering. We might disagree on other things, but we could always agree with what Mary had to say about mothering."

The revised manual was 166 pages long, printed in Janson type on 5½ x 8½ inch pages, and bound in blue cloth, with the title THE WOMANLY ART OF BREASTFEEDING in graceful white Lydian Cursive. As Betty pointed out, it was completed four years and ten babies from the day it was started.

Beginning To Organize Its Leaders

The founding mothers were not especially concerned about formal organization in the early years of the League. In fact, as Mary Ann Cahill recalled, they didn't have any plans at all to speak of, except to offer breastfeeding help to any woman who wanted it.

Vi Lennon well remembers her feelings about the League's future.

"I didn't ever see that this would be a big organization," she said. "I didn't see it as being that important or that it would catch on."

Once the League's growth required that the founding mothers begin to do some organizing, they made it as simple and as basic as possible. They wanted to be free to spend most of their time helping mothers, rather than overseeing administrative details.

"We said we weren't going to be bothered with an organizational structure," Betty said. "We kept saying we didn't want to get into a big organizational thing."

In the early years, the League's growth was slow but steady. Within only a few months after holding the first League meeting, there were so many women asking to come that it was necessary to split into two groups. Marian and Mary Ann Kerwin continued to lead the group at Mary White's house. Edwina, Betty, and Mary Ann Cahill began leading a second group at Edwina's house. (Vi Lennon was inactive as a leader at this time because of her distance from Franklin Park and the demands of her young family.)

Early in 1958 Gloria Watson, Dee Hoder, and Lucya Prince, who had attended several meetings in Franklin Park, wanted to start a group for their friends and neighbors in Chicago. The founding mothers agreed, and the third La Leche League group was born.

It was also in 1958 that the first group outside of the Chicago area was formed. Martha Pugacz of Cleveland, Ohio, had been considering starting a

> *"We didn't realize that they didn't have the same concept of mothering through breastfeeding that we had."*

group of some kind for nursing mothers when she heard about La Leche League. She was eager to start a League group in Cleveland to provide help for the mothers there, and again the founders gave their blessing. In less than a year and a half, the original Franklin Park group had multiplied into four.

An ever-increasing number of women with whom the founding mothers were corresponding began asking to start their own groups.

"We'd hear from these women from far away who said they wanted to join us, and we'd write back and say, 'Fine. Set up your own organization because we're not going to have a big organizational structure,'" Betty said. "So they would call themselves La Leche League, but then we discovered that they were saying things we didn't like hearing. For instance, they might be very nutritionally oriented, and this would be their whole thrust."

"Or they would be big on bottles," Edwina added. "They'd say, 'We're all for breastfeeding, but a mother has to get out, too,' so they would promote supplementary bottles.

"There were all kinds of things being said in the name of La Leche League," Edwina explained. "And it was our fault because we'd told them to go ahead and do what they wanted. We didn't realize that they didn't have the same concept of mothering through breastfeeding that we had. We realized we were going to have to put a stop to this, so we began qualifying leaders in and out of the area."

The job of qualifying leaders got under way in 1962 under the direction of Mary Jane Brizzolara. Mary Jane was one of the League's earliest members, and she recalls vividly the feelings she had after attending her first meeting in 1957.

"It was like coming home to mother," Mary Jane said. "I felt an instant rapport with every woman there. In those days, any woman who wanted to have her baby naturally and breastfeed it thought she was the only person in the world who wanted those things. But to go to that first meeting and discover a whole room full of women who had the same feelings and the same values—it was great."

Mary Jane recalled the problems she was faced with as she began the process of qualifying leaders.

"It was a question of how to maintain quality," Mary Jane explained. "If other people were going to be using our name, we had to come up with some kind of quality control to maintain the standards and philosophy that we started out with. We also had to be certain they were giving out correct breastfeeding information."

The solution Mary Jane arrived at was a questionnaire to be filled out by women wanting to start a La Leche group.

"The questionnaire was two or three pages with about fifteen questions," Mary Jane said. "Some of the questions required only very brief answers, and others were essay-type. Having the mothers fill out the questionnaire helped us to see any weak areas they might have so that we could give them help where they needed it."

Mary Jane recalled that there were two primary objectives in the leader qualification process.

"We wanted to convey the League attitude toward breastfeeding and being a mother," she said.

"And we wanted to supplement whatever knowledge the mothers had. People across the country had very little specific information about breastfeeding. But we had access to Dr. White and Dr. Ratner, and we supplied the mothers with a lot of information that couldn't be obtained anywhere else."

Mary Jane, who had eight children, resigned her position in 1964.

"I found it becoming more and more difficult to maintain my standards of mothering and do all of the things I needed to be doing to qualify leaders for League," Mary Jane said. "I saw that I wasn't able to handle both jobs, due to the ages and needs of my children at that time. In a way, it was a difficult decision to give up my marvelous involvement with the League, yet I knew that it was the right decision to put my family's needs first. I couldn't be preaching 'family first' and not living it."

Like so many others whose lives have been touched by La Leche League, Mary Jane recalled the magnitude of the impact that the League had on her life.

"What we learned from League was so much more than just the art of breastfeeding. We learned about human development. First the development of our babies, then our children, and finally of ourselves and the world and our place in it.

"Being part of the League was a major turningpoint in the lives of nearly all of us who were involved in the early years. It tremendously influenced our characters and our personality development. Through League, we found and adopted certain principles, and we lived our lives by them. I'm still living by those same principles today. La Leche League changed the course of my life. And it all started with the simple desire to learn how to nurse my baby!"

Finding A Symbol

Over the years, the La Leche logo has become an integral part of the League's identity. The beautiful simplicity of the mother cradling her baby in her arms conveys to all the League's message of love for the baby and the joy of mothering.

How ironic that none of the founders can quite remember how or when this beautiful symbol was chosen.

"The suggestion to have a logo came from outside," Edwina recalled. "Different women were telling us we should have one."

"We thought about having a symbol for a long time without doing anything about it," Marian said. Marian thinks it was probably Madge Bennett who persuaded the founders to begin looking in earnest for an official logo.

Madge was active in the League in the early 1960s, and was a member of the Executive Board. Late in 1964 she was put in charge of public relations and education for the League.

"She was young and blonde and pretty," Betty recalled, "and very vivacious and enthusiastic."

"Madge was very public relations oriented, and she thought we should have a symbol people would identify with the League," Marian said.

Mary Ann Cahill was the editor of the League NEWS when the search for a logo began in June of 1961. When the Arnolds began printing the NEWS in January of 1961, a sketch of a mother and baby was incorporated into the design of the nameplate. The founders decided that as long as they were going to use a logo, they might as well ask mothers to submit designs so that they could choose the most suitable one.

The first announcement of the search for an official logo was made in the June, 1961 NEWS:

La Leche League is looking for a sketch, to be used as its official symbol, that interprets the nursing mother of today. Since breastfeeding belongs to mothers in all parts of the world and is not limited by complexion or age or by social or economic status, the League is seeking a figure that expresses in simple lines the features that are common to all nursing mothers, such as maturity and a loving giving of self.

The search for a logo was a long and sometime frustrating one. Proposed logo designs appeared in the NEWS for the next year and a half. Mary Ann Cahill remembers some discouraging times.

"A lot of times it seemed like nobody else cared. Sometimes I wondered if the search was worth going on with," she said.

None of the founders can remember exactly how or when the logo was finally selected. Since it was used on the cover of the 1963 edition of THE WOMANLY ART OF BREASTFEEDING, it is assumed that the selection was made by early 1963.

"We must have voted on it because that's the way we did things," Marian said. "I think we must have all seen it and liked it and kind of said, 'That's it.'"

Of the many sketches that were submitted, it was Madge Bennett's design that was selected. It was not until the March/April, 1964 issue of the NEWS that the official announcement was made.

"In the last issue of the NEWS, Mrs. William Bennett of LaGrange, Ill., was pictured holding her bright-eyed baby, Alyssa Alexandra. Months ago, maybe even years by now, Madge submitted this symbol as her interpretation of La Leche League's nursing mother. It has become a favorite, adorning the NEWS, League stationery, and the cover of our manual, THE WOMANLY ART."

Madge Bennett's design has become so much a part of La Leche League's identity that it is hard to believe that the League existed for seven years without it.

39

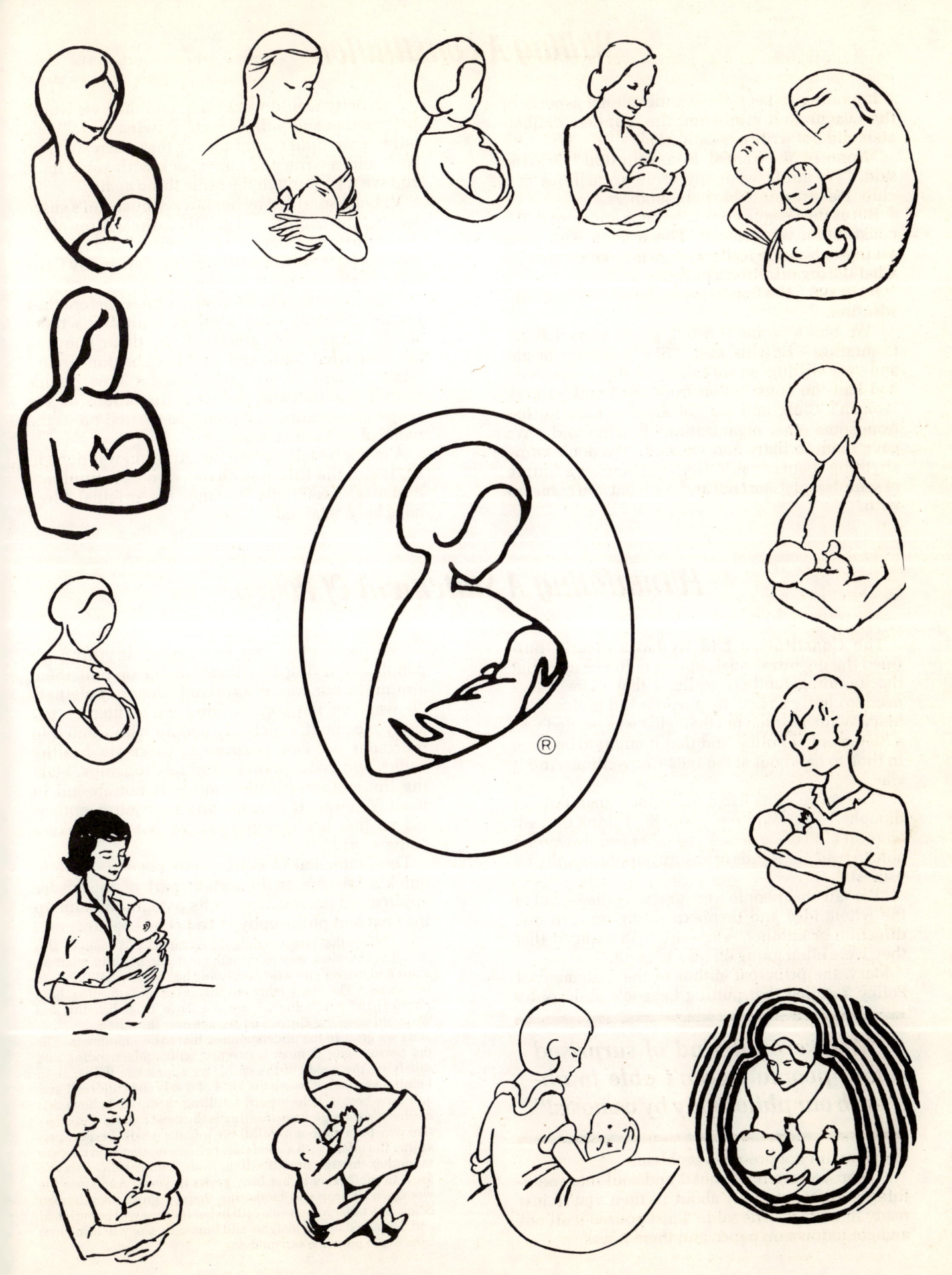

Writing A Constitution

Intending to keep the organizational aspects of the League to a minimum, the founders deliberately did not write a constitution.

"None of us wanted a constitution," Edwina said. "We didn't want any of the formalities of a club. We just wanted to help mothers."

But as the League grew, it became apparent that a constitution was needed. The women who were asking to become leaders needed to know exactly what the organization's purpose was.

So in 1963, the founders set about writing a constitution.

"We had a woman in our group named Betty Cummings," Edwina said. "She was very bright and very willing, so we asked her if she would do it. I had the constitution from the Franklin Park Women's Club, and we got another constitution from some other organization" Edwina said. "We gave them to Betty and we said, 'We don't know anything about constitutions, but here are a couple of samples. Just start out and see what you come up with.'

"So Betty would work on it, and then we would get together and pull it apart," Edwina said. "We'd tell her we didn't want this or that, then she'd go back and rewrite and come back with some more and we'd go through the same thing again."

Vi Lennon, aided by her lawyer-husband's sharp legal mind, contributed greatly to the writing of the constitution. Dozens of rewrites and several months later the Constitution and General By Laws of La Leche League were completed.

"The Constitution let mothers know before they became leaders what kind of limitations there were," Edwina explained. "It let them know in advance what could and could not be done in our name. It laid down guidelines for how groups should function and put clear limitations on the scope of activities that could be carried on in the name of La Leche League."

A major revision of the Constitution was done in 1971, and the title was changed to Constitutional By-Laws. Essentially, though, the original ideas have been retained.

Formulating A Statement Of Policy

The Constitution and By-Laws clearly outlined the organizational aspects of the League, but the founding mothers realized that there was a need to clarify La Leche's purpose and philosophy. Mary White pointed out that what was needed was a Statement of Policy, and that it ought to be done in time to hand out at the 1964 Convention. And it was.

"The seven of us had a marvelous unanimity of thought," Mary White explained. "I think that we were all kind of surprised that other people weren't able to read our minds or absorb our philosophy by osmosis!

"We saw that people were grasping the kernel of the whole idea and then expanding on it in one direction or another," she said. "We realized that they were often going off on a tangent."

Mary, the principal author of the Statement of Policy, recalled that putting League's philosophy

> **"We were all kind of surprised that people weren't able to absorb our philosophy by osmosis!"**

on paper did not present a problem.

"When you are really heart and soul into something and feel strongly about it, then you're just ready to write it," she said. "I just poured it all out and got it down on paper, and there it was.

"We weren't trying to impose anything on people, or trying to educate them or pull them around to our way of thinking," Mary explained. "It was just the sort of thing we wanted to tell everyone about, especially people who wanted to represent us. Our purpose is to create healthy babies and good mother-child relationships. Making the mother a better mother is not an end in itself. You want to help her do a good job of mothering so that her children can go out and make a better world."

The Statement of Policy, four pages in length, quickly became an important part of the leader application process. Two of its paragraphs sum up the goal and philosophy of La Leche League:

> We believe that breastfeeding is best for baby. We believe also that it is the ideal way to initiate good parent-child relationships and to strengthen the family and hence the whole fabric of our society. The many other advantages of breastfeeding, both physical and psychological, are in a sense fringe benefits, and we avoid stressing any one advantage over the others.
>
> As we grow in the understanding that to be a mother is to be the person who is most concerned with understanding and satisfying the needs of the child, we appreciate the value of helping each other to see the kind of needs our children have, and how best to help toward fulfilling them. We believe that mothering through breastfeeding is the most natural and effective way for a mother to fulfill the infant's needs. Besides providing the infant with a good start in life, a mother who chooses to mother through breastfeeding, finds it an excellent way to grow in mothering as her baby grows in years. And since the woman who grows in mothering thereby grows as a human being, any other role she may fill in her lifetime will be enriched and deepened by the insights and humanity she will bring to it from her experience as a mother.

Becoming International

As the League continued to grow and spread, the name of La Leche League of Franklin Park, Inc., became too limiting and confusing. It was awkward to have both the individual Franklin Park groups and the organization as a whole using "Franklin Park" as part of their names. And the inclusion of "Franklin Park" in the official name seemed less and less appropriate as groups from across the country and around the world came under League's umbrella.

On June 2, 1964, the name of the organization was officially changed to La Leche League International, Inc. At that time there were 115 groups in the United States and 6 in foreign countries.

From one group in Franklin Park to 121 groups around the world — the founding mothers never dreamed what kind of a need they were filling when they invited their friends to Mary White's home that October night in 1956.

Holding A Convention

As the founders corresponded with mothers in other areas who had started League groups, these mothers often expressed their wish to get together and meet personally with the founding mothers. The founders always brushed the idea aside. After all, who ever heard of mothers and babies getting on trains and planes and buses to travel to a meeting?

"Tom Kerwin was something of a prophet," Vi Lennon recalled. "We were having a meeting at the Kerwins one night in 1959, and Tom said that someday we were going to gather everyone together at a convention and talk over our ideas. It struck me so funny—I got a mental picture of a lot of mothers and babies getting off an airplane to come to a meeting. I thought it was hilarious!"

But in 1962 the founders finally began giving serious thought to having a convention. "The mothers from other states were really putting pressure on us to have one," Edwina recalled.

And Mary Jane Brizzolara was pushing hard for a convention too. After working on qualifying leaders for over a year, she was convinced of the necessity for a convention.

"She was the one who said, 'We just can't have these women all over the country representing La Leche League without really understanding what we are all about.'" Edwina recalled. "She said we'd have to have everyone come together and get everything straight so they would understand exactly what they were representing."

Finally convinced of the value of a convention, the founders set June of 1964 as the date and began planning. The Knickerbocker Hotel in downtown Chicago was selected to host the convention, and Nell Ryan was made convention chairman.

"Nell was actively working in a group at the time," Edwina said. "She was very articulate, very capable, and obviously good at organizing. We had no previous experience whatsoever with conventions, so Nell had to pioneer all the way. She really did a bang-up job for us."

Edwina recalls the day they went down to the Knickerbocker to begin to make the initial arrangements.

"I remember we were scared stiff that nobody would show up," she said. "The manager wanted us to give him an estimate — how many did we think would come? We said we'd never done this before so we didn't know. He asked for lots of facts and figures that we didn't have because we weren't in the habit of keeping facts and figures.

"'About how many mothers do you hear from?' he asked.

"'Oh, *lots!*' we said. 'But after all, these would be *mothers* who would be coming, and they would be coming from *out of town*, and it would cost them *money*, so we would probably be lucky if we had fifty.'

" He said, 'Well, let's put down seventy-five.'

"Then we talked some more and he said, 'I'm going to put down a round figure of one hundred and fifty.'"

> *"I got a mental picture of a lot of mothers and babies getting off a plane to come to a meeting. I thought it was hilarious!"*

Still wondering whether anyone at all would really come, the founders and Nell Ryan got busy sending out letters announcing the convention. Then they began lining up speakers.

"We didn't pay them because we didn't have any money to pay them with," Edwina said. "They were all people we knew, and we just told them that it was our first convention and we didn't have any money and would they do it for us? One doctor got another doctor, and that's the way it went.

"The hotel manager was terrific with us," Edwina recalled. "He was very helpful and very patient and very accommodating. The things we asked for were totally different from what a hotel had ever been asked for before. We needed diaper containers in every room, and cribs, and a rock and rest room. We were very apologetic about all these things we needed, but the manager said, 'Listen, when the businessmen come, *they* want a bar in every room and ice on tap. Your requests are a little different, but nothing we can't handle.'"

Edwina remembers the excitement she felt when she arrived at the hotel the night before the convention opened.

"It was exciting just being downtown," she said. "None of us had done that sort of thing for years. It was a big event for the family to have dinner in the hotel dining room. Then we went upstairs, and John and the boys installed me in my room. It was exciting and strange, and a little bit scary, too. You were always afraid you were spending more than you were aware of, and that suddenly someone would hand you a horrible bill that you wouldn't have the money to pay for."

The big day came at last, and not fifty, or seventy-five, or one hundred and fifty, but four hundred and twenty-five mothers with one hundred babies descended on the Knickerbocker. The founders were astonished. They never dreamed that so many mothers would think it was worth the trouble and expense to come. The gratitude and enthusiasm of the mothers at that first convention were simply overwhelming.

"The first convention was terribly exciting because it was the first time we had all been together to share these ideas," Edwina explained. "Everybody was so glad to find everybody else. We were alone in our thinking in those days. Anybody who had a philosophy like ours was alone in her environment. The mothers at the convention kept saying, 'To think I'm here talking about nursing and nobody is laughing!'

"And of course it was the first time they had heard doctors getting up and supporting this thinking. They couldn't believe their ears when they heard *M.D.s* openly supporting the ideals in which they so firmly believed."

The keynote speaker was Dr. Herbert Ratner, who gave a memorable speech on the importance of being a mother. Charlotte Aiken, editor of the *Child-Family Digest* that had given the founders so much inspiration, was there as an honored guest.

Most of the sessions were held in the Knickerbocker's ballroom. The speakers were at one end with chairs in front of the platform, and all along the back there were mothers and babies and rocking chairs and blankets. The people in the front were able to hear, and the mothers in the back had plenty of freedom with their babies.

"It was a very select group who came to that first convention," Edwina recalled. "They were the pioneers. They were the ones to whom all of this was so important, and they were so starved for this information. They would have moved heaven and earth to get there. Nobody was paying their way. There was no such thing as your area organization paying your way. They were all there on their own funds. Many of them had really scrimped and saved for it. Many had asked for the trip as a birthday or Christmas present and promised not to ask for anything else for five years if only they could go to the convention.

"So many of them wrote to us later and said that their husbands had said that sending them to the convention had paid for itself time and time again because of the tremendous change that had taken place in the mother and then ultimately in the whole family."

The first convention in 1964 was the first time League mothers had all been together to share their ideas.

Appointing An Executive Coordinator

La Leche League groups began springing up across the country in ever-increasing numbers in the early 1960s. Mothers in distant areas who found the breastfeeding help they had been searching for through the League wanted to start League groups in their towns to provide help for their friends and neighbors. The first women who wanted to start League groups would correspond with one of the founding mothers, who would answer any breastfeeding questions that the new leader had.

By 1962 they had put Mary Jane Brizzolara in charge of approving new leaders. When Mary Jane saw that these leaders needed continuing contact as their groups developed, she asked Alice Dillon and others to help her keep in touch with them.

This initial system of providing help for potential leaders and new groups was relatively unstructured. Mary Jane and her assistants learned as they went along, and often had to guess what these women needed and how they could provide it.

"It was the 1964 convention that made the founders see the need to really organize all those groups and leaders," Judy Torgus said.

Judy was one of the League's early and enthusiastic supporters.

"I remember so well the first meeting she attended in the fall of 1959," Edwina recalled. "She was so young and pretty, and she was expecting her first baby in a few weeks. She was going to have a natural delivery with Dr. White and breastfeed the baby, and I remember thinking how marvelous that someone so young was doing everything just right the way Judy was."

Judy lost no time in offering to be of service to

"These women had a deep commitment to League, and they needed far more help than they had previously been given."

League in any way she could. She began almost immediately to work as a letter writer, answering mothers who had written to the League for help. She began leading a group in 1961, and was one of the original chapter presidents.

Judy attended the 1964 convention, and remembers the founding mothers' reaction to the overwhelming turnout — their astonishment at the number of mothers who cared enough to come. She said that meeting all these women at the convention convinced the founders of two things: that these women had a deep commitment to League, and that they needed far more help than they had previously been given.

At the time of the convention, there were one hundred and twenty-one La Leche League groups. It was evident that the seven founding mothers couldn't possibly take care of the needs of so many groups, and that some system should be devised to provide the necessary help.

The Executive Board therefore created the position of Executive Coordinator and appointed Judy Torgus to fill it. When she became Executive Coordinator in July of 1964, Judy became responsible for the functioning of all League groups and leaders.

She saw that delegating was an immediate necessity, and her first task was to appoint a state coordinator for each of the states that had a sufficient number of groups.

"We wanted to set up people within the states who were experienced and could guide the newer

"In the beginning, the function of the state coordinator was to keep in touch with every group in her state."

people coming in," Judy explained. There were about fifteen states at that time with enough groups to need a coordinator. Some of the early state coordinators were Martha Pugacz in Ohio, Judy Sobel in New Jersey, Betty Ann Countryman in Indiana, and Nell Ryan in Illinois.

Leaders' letters began springing up almost as soon as states got coordinators.

"The first letter was usually just an announcement saying, 'I'm your new state coordinator,'" Judy said. "But then the coordinators found it was an effective way to communicate with all of the leaders in the state.

"I corresponded with and got meeting reports from all of the groups in states that didn't have a state coordinator. There was a lot of work to do because this was the first time any of them had been told that they were expected to send in meeting reports.

"The biggest problem I had in the beginning was getting leaders to limit their meetings to the acceptable material," Judy recalled. "They wanted to bring in speakers and films, things like that.

"And I spent a lot of time clarifying philosophy for the leaders. That was always of primary importance, because it was the leaders who interpreted League philosophy to the mothers in their groups."

The new state coordinators encountered numerous problems as they began setting up their state organizations. In order to provide the coordinators with assistance and guidance, a State Coordinators' meeting was held in Chicago in July of 1967. The twenty state coordinators found the meeting so helpful that they requested that conferences be held at regular intervals. Thereafter, coordinators' conferences became yearly events.

Judy handled the job of Executive Coordinator alone until 1967, when she asked Ruth Ann Selvey to be her assistant. By 1968 Ruth Ann had more work than she could handle, so she brought in Diane Kramer to help.

Ruth Ann and Diane became acting coordinators for states that did not have their own coordinators, each of them acting as coordinator for half of these states.

"By 1970 there was more work than the three of us could handle, so I called a special meeting," Judy said. "I had a huge map of the United States on the wall, and I told them we were going to parcel it all out and put every state under a coordinator." In some cases two neighboring states that each had a small number of League groups were joined under one coordinator.

"In the beginning, the function of the coordinator was to keep in touch with every group in her state," Judy explained. But as states got more and more groups, it became impossible for the coordinator to keep up with all of them.

"One of our first thoughts was to cut down on the coordinators' load by going to series (once every four months) reports," Judy said. "We were aware right from the beginning that handling a meeting report from every League group every month was going to become overwhelming."

Several states tried series reports, but the system didn't work out as expected.

"We left it up to the state coordinators, and as things progressed, almost all of them found that monthly reports worked best. They felt that they had better communication with the leader when she wrote once a month rather than only once a series," Judy said.

So the original organizational plans were reversed. Rather than eliminating reports, personnel were added. In the larger states, assistant state coordinators came into being to help handle all of the paperwork.

Eventually, some states found even this arrangement inadequate. Ohio was the first state to have one hundred groups, and they faced administrative problems keeping up with that many. They set up a new organizational structure to meet those needs by developing a system of Districts within the state. As the number of LLL groups grew in other states, they, too, developed a system, such as Districts, to meet their needs.

State Meetings began to evolve in 1968. The Executive Board asked Diane Kramer to be in charge of this new aspect of LLL. Eventually, she developed guidelines for them. "State Meetings developed out of a real need for leaders to meet with one another and share ideas," Judy recalled. "At first, they were just informal get-togethers. Eventually, they became more organized, involving larger groups of people."

Judy Torgus served as Executive Coordinator for twelve years, until 1976, when the department was reorganized.

"Judy was the right person at the right time," Edwina said. "She had just the right abilities for the job that needed to be done. She had talent, capability, and generosity, the kind of qualities that built La Leche League."

Appointing A Director Of New Group Chairmen

Following the 1964 convention, the job of approving La Leche League leaders was taken over by Marybeth Doucette. Marybeth attended her first League meeting in October of 1959. She was new in town, saw a notice in the newspaper about the meeting, and since she was nursing a newborn, her fourth, she thought it would be nice to meet some other nursing mothers. She came to the meeting, leaving her four-week-old baby at home! But Marybeth soaked up the League philosophy like a sponge, and baby Jeanne came right along to the next meeting.

Marybeth quickly became active in the organization. She took over the NEWS subscriptions in 1961, and it was there that her phenomenal ability for organization came to the founding mothers' attention.

Marybeth was given the title of Director of New Groups in 1964, and she immediately began adding to the requirements for leadership.

"The whole program just evolved," Marybeth explained. "It used to be that when a woman wanted to start a group we said, 'Good. Here's your badge (leader's card), here's your group, we'll put you in our directory.' It hadn't been terribly organized because the people who were doing it were busy being mothers. But as the League grew, we saw that it needed a little more order and a little more plan to it."

One of the first things Marybeth and her assistants did was to introduce a resumé to learn more about the applicant's nursing experiences and attitudes.

"We slowly found that they should have nursed a

baby by LLL standards," Marybeth explained. "They couldn't be very helpful to other mothers if they'd nursed a baby every four hours for six weeks and then put the baby on a bottle.

"Some of the applicants had nursed a baby successfully but didn't have the thorough knowledge of breastfeeding we felt they should have before they tried to help others. So we began questioning what they had read," Marybeth said.

"Then we needed to know how they were relating to the people they were dealing with. Some had the information and had nursed their babies, but couldn't put it across in a group discussion manner."

Determining whether an applicant had the necessary qualifications for League leadership was difficult and time consuming because everything had to be done through the mail. All applicants were approved through a Chicago-based New Group Chairman.

"There were no state-level people, no state meetings, and no funds for travel," Marybeth explained. "We had an extended discourse by mail with each leader applicant until we really established whether or not she understood what we were reaching for and wanted her to impart to others. We wanted her to both understand the nursing techniques and grasp the League mothering philosophy."

Marybeth estimated that the application process usually took between six months and a year.

By early 1966 Marybeth began appointing state-level New Group Chairmen. When a state had a large number of mothers applying for leadership and when there was someone in the state who was experienced and well versed in League philosophy, then that state got a New Group Chairman. By 1972, when Marybeth resigned, every state in the United States had its own New Group Chairman and all applications were being processed on the state level.

"Marybeth had a tremendous capacity for the kind of work she did, and great convictions about the importance of our mothering philosophy," Edwina said. "She devoted a tremendous amount of time to her job because she was committed to spreading our philosophy of mothering."

Marybeth saw several changes in leaders in the eight years that she directed the leader applicant program.

"Leaders began having longer nursing experiences," Marybeth said. "They were supported by knowing other people who were doing it, too. The NEWS, conventions, state meetings, all had helped a great deal. The additional publications we got out helped, too.

"Leaders also became more well read," she said. "In the beginning it was basically our manual and Karen Pryor and that was it." But as League materials and other related materials increased, leaders had far greater enrichment possibilities.

With longer nursing experiences, extensive reading, and more contact with other nursing mothers, the leader was much better able to be really helpful in meeting another mother's needs, Marybeth said.

Marybeth believes that a woman's mothering experience influences what she brings to League leadership.

"Mothering is learned, developed, perfected, and made much more beautiful by experience," Marybeth said. "Many women don't see what total mothering really is until they have had a least two or three children. All of a sudden all of the pieces seem to come together, and they are much more mature in their mothering and able to reach out and help other mothers much more effectively."

Expanding Its Office Space

The founders had barely gotten their headquarters moved from Edwina's dining room to their new office before they outgrew it. Two desks and a filing cabinet filled it to capacity. In September of 1963, six months after they had moved in, they moved down the hall to their second office, about three times the size of the original one.

The new office was staffed by Betty, Edwina, and stenographer LaVerne Spadaro. The extra space was well worth the higher rent, $75.00 a month.

In January of 1965 Mrs. Charles Leonard, Marian Tompson's mother, was hired to take charge of the 5,000 NEWS subscriptions. The office was once again becoming crowded—with four desks, filing cabinets, and boxes and boxes of manuals and reprints there was very little room left for the people.

But it was a more urgent problem than overcrowding that prompted the founders to begin looking for their third office.

"The big problem with our second office was that it was on the second floor," Edwina explained. "We had a lot of trouble getting delivery on our manual because the truck drivers' union would not permit them to carry the books upstairs. They just unloaded them on the sidewalk outside. We were constantly pleading with them to help us because the boxes were too heavy for us to carry up a flight of steps, and some of the drivers were kind and helped us. But when we realized they wouldn't be covered by their insurance if anything happened while they were carrying the boxes upstairs, we decided we couldn't do that anymore. We didn't know what we were going to do because we couldn't haul those boxes up those steep stairs ourselves. That made it urgent that we get a main floor office."

So the search for an office was on—again.

La Leche League's First — and

Dr. Herbert Ratner

Dr. Herbert Ratner's influence has been subtle, but his impact profound. It would be difficult to overestimate the significance of his contributions to La Leche League.

He is totally supportive of breastfeeding. But it is his respect for nature, his dedication to home and family, and his philosophy of life that have contributed so much to the League.

"He made me feel that I, as a mother, had a tremendously important contribution to make to my own family and to society," Edwina said. "He said that good mothers were the basis for a good society. He felt that to shortchange a baby was to do a tremendous disservice to yourself, the baby, and society."

Dr. Ratner believes that the family is the foundation of a healthy society, and he is deeply concerned about what he sees happening in America today.

"There is no other way of turning out mature adults with more certainty or with more effectiveness."

But the home is no longer the center of life in America, and Dr. Ratner feels that society has grievously suffered because of it.

"We know that something has gone wrong," he said. "Alienation, psychiatric illness, suicide — all the indices of a sick society have increased. We no longer have the example of fidelity — the road to happiness — when the home is no longer central. Part of the problem is that parents forget the heritage that had benefited them, so they don't pass it on," he said. "Parents who came from a home where their parents stayed home to serve their needs grew up with more security, but when grown up forgot the parental dedication which served them so well. They mistakenly attribute their stability and their own children's instability to external factors. That's why we have to educate future and present parents. One didn't have to tell mothers or grandmothers how important the first three years are. They knew that. They would laugh that today one has to prove that the child needs the mother totally, so to speak, the first three years. But we get exposed to alternatives, and the alternatives are seductive."

Why did breastfeeding get lost?

"There are many reasons, but one reason is the notion that breastfeeding ties the woman down," he said. "Women figured that with bottle feeding

Drs. Ratner and White at the Whites' Franklin Park house, 1958.

they'd be liberated. They became vulnerable to other persuasions. they ended up thinking of the baby as one who only needs diaper changing, feeding, and sleeping.

"Past generations didn't think in these terms," he said. "They lived daily in an intimate relationship. They went to bed together, got up together, ate together, played and prayed together. Bonding occurred from birth spontaneously, in depth, and possessed permanency.

continued on page 48

Foremost — Medical Advisors
Dr. Gregory White

It was the era of wonder drugs, a time when doctors and laymen alike believed that drugs were the answer to nearly any problem. Antibiotics were requested and prescribed freely in the 1950s. Belief in the nearly miraculous powers of doctors and their medicines was at an all-time high.

Yet there was a doctor who, though he was young and quite new to the practice of medicine, had a different perspective on health care. His most frequent prescription could not be filled by any druggist. The prescription was patience and love, and the doctor was Gregory J. White.

Drs. Ratner and White at the Whites' home in River Forest, 1975.

"The 1950s was an era when people went to the doctor all the time," Edwina explained. "Whenever the least little thing was wrong, you called the doctor and got an antibiotic. If the baby was sick, the hospital was considered the best place for him.

"But Dr. White was just the opposite," Edwina continued. "He would say, 'In this case the child doesn't really need an antibiotic, Mother. He just needs lots of rest and keep him as quiet as you can.' Mothers liked antibiotics because they thought the child might be up and around again fast. But Dr. White would say, 'I'd like to give nature a chance first. It may take a little longer, but in the long run it will be better.'

"When a mother would ask Dr. White whether a child should be hospitalized, he would say, 'The baby is sick, but in this case there isn't anything they can do for him in the hospital that you can't do better at home. The nurse wouldn't be able to soothe and carefully watch him the way you can!'"

In an era when mothers were counseled to let the baby cry it out, and warned about the dire consequences of spoiling their infants, Dr. White was advising mothers to offer their babies large doses of tender loving care.

Dr. White's approach to childbirth, too, was unlike that of most other doctors. In the 1950s mothers were anesthetized for delivery and confined to their hospital beds for an extended time following childbirth. New mothers were regarded as sick people who needed intensive hospital care.

But when Dr. White was the attending physician, childbirth became an experience to be treasured, rather than an ordeal to be dreaded. His understanding of a woman's unique needs at this special time in her life, coupled with his belief that nature intended women to experience and enjoy giving birth, allowed childbirth to be a beautiful and enriching occasion. For Dr. White's patients, there was joy and fulfillment in what other doctors had turned into a dreaded procedure.

Dr. White didn't feel that his job was over once the baby had been brought into the world. He instilled in his new mothers a sense of pride in the importance of their role as mothers and confidence in their ability to handle it.

"He made you feel so good about becoming a mother," Edwina said. "He started during pregnancy to give you confidence that you would be able to handle your future role as a mother. He made you feel that babies were a very special bless-

Dr. Ratner continued from page 46

"Research today demonstrates what fools we have been. In order to get back to where we were, it seems as if we now have to prove the verity of the truths that nature has always made freely available to us whenever we extended open arms to receive them."

Dr. Ratner's support of home births is another aspect of his belief that home should be central, and where significant human events should take place.

"In a home birth, the mother is the queen bee," he said. "In a hospital birth, the mother is a transient boarder lowest on the totem pole. In a home birth, the mother and baby begin their love relationship unencumbered by strangers; mother wants baby, baby wants mother, and like a couple on a honeymoon they have each other to themselves.

"In hospitals," Dr. Ratner continued, "separation of mother and baby following birth is like separation of bride and groom following marriage. It's like going to a hotel on one's honeymoon and being isolated from one another for hygienic or other reasons, only permitting contact on a four-hour schedule.

"The more we study it, the more we find out how important the baby's and mother's first hours and days are." Dr. Ratner firmly believes that "mothers and babies are in reality a couplet as in pregnancy, that nature abhors a separation, and that the mass nursery is a displaced person's concentration camp."

He also believes that parenthood brings growth dependent baby necessitates total unselfishness. In the process one becomes a better person. and maturity.

"Going from the single state to the married state is one step," he said. "Going from being husband and wife to being father and mother is another step. We can no longer indulge in moments of selfishness as we can with another adult. The completely

"Parenting, then, is a matter of maturing. What few realize is that while parents mature children, children mature parents even more."

"Motherhood is an opportunity for growth. Three children nurture motherhood more than one. Each mothering experience enriches."

"Parenting, then, is a matter of maturing. What few realize is that while parents mature children, children mature parents even more. One doesn't become a mother overnight. Like childhood and even adulthood, motherhood is a state that hopefully continues to mature one until death."

Dr. White continued from page 47

ing and that it was terribly exciting and wonderful that you were going to have a baby, whether it was your first or your tenth."

It comes as no surprise that Dr. White was one of the few doctors in the 1950s who had successful nursing mothers in his practice. He offered large doses of encouragement, and he recognized the unique advantages of mother-to-mother help.

"A person who is in a situation has more feeling for it than someone who never has been and never can be," he explained, "so I had nursing mothers helping each other on an informal basis."

It was Dr. White's positive, encouraging approach to helping mothers that provided the model for the founding mothers as they began helping other women.

"No matter what you would call him about, he was always so calm," Edwina said, "and he would always end the conversation on a positive note — 'You're doing a great job, Mother!' I was always floating when I hung up after talking to him. When I began counseling other nursing mothers, I always tried to remember how good he made me feel about the job I was doing and to make the mothers who called me feel the same way."

Having observed the encouraging rate of success through mother-to-mother help in his practice, Dr. White had good reason to feel confident that La Leche League's approach to helping mothers was the right one. The surprise was the astounding response to the League's offer of help.

"I thought they would be a nice little local group," Dr. White said. "I thought, 'They'll help fifteen or twenty mothers, and it will be great!'"

But though its intentions were modest and its goals limited, La Leche League thrived and grew. Dr. White has some ideas why.

"It might have happened anywhere else, and in fact there were several groups for nursing mothers that started at about the same time. But many of these other groups were a product of doctors and nurses rather than mothers themselves. They were professionals teaching, rather than mothers helping mothers, and these groups stayed small.

"The times and the women came together," Dr. White said of the League. "La Leche League succeeded because there were a number of women interested in helping other nursing mothers who happened to live close together and who worked harmoniously together," he said. "And they succeeded because all of them felt that the cause was more important than personalities."

Dr. White sees group support as one of the most important things LLL provides. "We're all social animals," he said. "We tend to move with the crowd. If the crowd were going in the right direction, that would be great. But ever since Adam bit the apple, there have been so many crowds going in wrong directions that following the crowd is usually not the thing to do.

"One of the big advantages of the League is not only the information you get, but the spoken support. The mother thinks, 'Gee, here are a bunch of nice people who do the same thing I do. I'm normal.' It's awfully hard to go it alone against everyone. It's much easier when you get some like-minded people together."

Is there really a significant difference between the nursing mother and the bottle-feeding mother? After spending thirty years watching the families in his practice grow up, Dr. White feels he is in a position to know. And his answer is a resounding, "Yes!"

"Ideally, parenthood is a very maturing experience," he said. "Getting off to a good start at it is very important. The mother who is nursing is much more in tune with her baby, and this carries through the rest of the child's life.

"The mother is enormously influenced and developed by the breastfeeding relationship, even on a physical basis. The mother who bottlefeeds doesn't have high prolactin levels, and doesn't have the same physical feelings toward her baby. She's handicapped. If she had a good mother and a good grandmother and was brought up with her motherly feelings encouraged, she may turn out to be a pretty good mother. But she could have been a lot better mother if she had breastfed."

Issuing A Leaders' Publication

The first issue of LEAVEN, La Leche League's bimonthly leaders' publication, appeared in the fall of 1965. The name "Leaven" was contributed by Mary Ann Cahill, and in the first issue Marian described its purpose: "To raise our sights and our hopes 'at home'...directed to women and kitchens which are often a League mother's office. It's bound to improve with kneading and punches!"

The International logo — the League symbol superimposed upon the world—was first used on the maiden issue of LEAVEN. Edwina was LEAVEN's first editor.

"As we got more leaders in other states it was very difficult to keep up with all of the correspondence," Edwina explained. "There was a need to communicate with our leaders about things we had learned and mistakes we wanted them to avoid. We needed a place where we could talk about how to improve meetings and call attention to the latest research. We felt that putting it all down in a paper of some kind seemed the best way to do it."

Prior to the development of LEAVEN the Executive Board had mailed out the minutes of its meet-

> **"To raise our sights and our hopes 'at home'. It's bound to improve with kneading and punches."**

ings to leaders in other areas in an effort to keep them up to date.

"A lot of things discussed at the Executive Board Meetings were things we felt the people in the field needed to know about, so we sent out the Board minutes," Edwina explained. "But then we decided that if we had a publication especially for the leaders, it would take care of those things they needed to know."

Originally LEAVEN was sent out to any interested League mothers as well as to leaders. It was issued irregularly in the early years. There was a full year between the first and second issues. The third issue followed six months later, and the fourth issue didn't appear until December of 1967. But with the fifth issue, in March of 1968, LEAVEN became a regular bimonthly publication sent free

> **"The International logo – the League symbol with the world superimposed upon it – was first used on the maiden issue of LEAVEN."**

to leaders only; printing and postage costs forced the Board to set a subscription price of $1.00 a year to others who wished to receive it.

NEWS Editor Nell Ryan was given a second hat as editor of LEAVEN and since then the two publications have always been edited by the same person—Lana Auriemma and Melanie Tompson during the interim between Nell and Mary Carson.

LEAVEN has developed as a forum for a variety of topics — suggestions for solving breastfeeding problems, ideas on effective meeting techniques, answers to attacks on breastfeeding from the media, and announcements of new reprints and other items available from LLLI.

Marian sees LEAVEN as serving two primary functions for leaders today—information and inspiration.

"Years ago a leader didn't have to keep up to date," Marian said, "because there wasn't much to keep up to date on. Today there is new information being published all the time that she needs to know about.

"It also helps her to work more effectively as a League leader," Marian said, "and gives her the inspiration she needs to effectively help the mothers who seek her guidance."

Moving...Again

La Leche League International found its third (and so far, final) home in August of 1965. It is across the street from the building where the first two offices were located. It originally consisted of two offices, a shipping room and a storage room. The 1200 square feet rented for $175.00 a month. Most important, it offered the badly needed ground-floor location.

Acquisition of the new office was cause for rejoicing at the Tompson household, as reported in the first issue of LEAVEN:

We've emptied the Tompson's garage of manuals, reprints, etc. Now they can get their car in again and Daddy Tompson is happy. Marian is smiling broadly over getting the NEWS file cabinets and addressograph out of their bedrooms...And the whole family is cheering, knowing that future issues of the NEWS will no longer be sorted in their living and dining rooms. We now have a long, long counter top built in at the office to handle NEWS sorting every other month, and to handle also the daily mailings which include well over 1,000 books a month.

Best of all, there were no steps to climb with the many thousands of manuals that were being delivered to the office door.

Gathering In Indianapolis

The first La Leche League convention in 1964 was so enthusiastically received that the founding mothers decided to hold another one in 1966. This time they moved the convention out of Chicago, to Indianapolis.

"We thought it would be a good idea to have it someplace besides Chicago," Edwina explained. "We had some very active groups in Indianapolis, and Betty Ann Countryman was there. We asked her to be the convention chairman and she enlisted the help of Dave Bosworth."

Unfortunately, Indianapolis proved to be a difficult place to fly into, necessitating plane changes for many mothers.

A second, and bigger, problem plagued the 1966 convention.

"The hotel didn't believe it when we told them to expect at least four hundred," Edwina recalled. "They hadn't saved rooms for all of the people who had reservations, let alone some extra rooms for the mothers who decided at the last minute to come. Over seven hundred people came, so there were hundreds of people who couldn't stay at the hotel and had to be put up at other hotels. I'll never forget being down in that lobby with my mouth open as they were saying, 'No rooms.' I couldn't believe that hotels ever did that."

The French translation of the manual by Canadian LLLers was hot off the press and made its debut at the convention.

This was also the year that dozens of strollers at the meal functions created such a hazard in the dining rooms that the founding mothers deemed it nothing short of a miracle that no baby was hurt as the waiters with loaded trays tried their best to serve the crowds. Since then no strollers or buggies of any kind have been permitted in the dining rooms or restaurants at the conventions.

It was in Indianapolis that Dr. Ratner in his keynote talk said that the role of the woman was to teach others the importance of love, and, prophetically perhaps, stressed the importance of the face-to-face relationship between mother and baby.

Urbane and witty psychiatrist Dr. John Nurnberger, in his banquet address titled, 'Love

The 1966 convention, held in Indianapolis.

That Man,' pointed out that maternal nurturing occurs in a special climate created by husband and wife, a climate in which the mother-child relationship can flourish.

Many other speakers and panels contributed to the flow of wit and wisdom, and when it was all over Convention participants left for home exhilarated, inspired, and eager to share all that they had learned and experienced.

...And Again In Denver

The decision to hold the 1968 LLLI Convention in Denver was made on the back stairs of the Sheraton Hotel in Indianapolis during the 1966 convention.

"There weren't enough elevators to accommodate the crowds at the Sheraton Hotel," Edwina explained, "so we were constantly walking up eight and ten flights of back stairs. As we were trudging up the stairs at one point with Dr. Robert Bradley, he said to us, 'I've been telling our bunch that we should have the next convention in Denver.' We knew that League in Denver was very enthusiastic and very capable, and it was then and there that we first considered holding the next convention there."

The 1968 LLLI Convention was indeed held in Denver, with Anne and Don Theobald as chairmen.

"It was a delightful convention," Edwina recalled. "We were in the brand new Hilton and we had oodles of room."

Some thousand mothers accompanied by five hundred babies were officially welcomed by Denver resident and founding mother Mary Ann Kerwin.

"I delivered the general welcome with two-month old John in my arms," Mary Ann said. "Only in La Leche League could a woman comfortably address such a crowd with a baby in her arms!"

Banquet speaker Ashley Montagu delighted the audience with a speech that was tremendously supportive of breastfeeding and mothers. "At the center of humanity will always stand the breastfeeding, loving mother."

It was at the Denver Convention that Marian announced that a "Salute to La Leche League," written by Dr. Lee Forrest Hill, the president of the American Academy of Pediatrics, had been published in the *Journal of Pediatrics*.

LLLI Medical Advisory Board member Dr. Mark Thoman had been a student of Dr. Hill's, and told him about La Leche League.

"Many doctors were brushing us aside as a general nuisance," Edwina said, "and Mark Thoman had suggested to Dr. Hill that something should be written about the good that the League had done. 'The doctors are failing the women and so these women are helping each other,' he told Dr. Hill. 'Let's not be giving them a black eye about it—let's praise them.'

"It was such a thrill to be in the *Journal of Pediatrics*," Edwina recalled. "We couldn't believe it. There it was in print—a *salute* to La Leche League. I remember saying to Marian just before she announced it at the Convention, 'I really think we've reached our zenith now. We have probably reached everybody who needs to be reached. The doctors will change and La Leche League won't be needed any more and we can fold up our tents and go home.'"

On that happy note the convention ended. But far from fading away into the night, La Leche League's star was steadily growing brighter and brighter.

Raising The Roof

La Leche League was growing at a phenomenal rate. The number of groups doubled from 150 to 300 in 1965, and NEWS subscriptions doubled in 1966 from 4,649 to 8,589. It quickly became apparent that the office space was going to have to grow, too.

There were two offices sharing the front portion of the ground floor with La Leche League at 9616 Minneapolis Avenue. As they became vacant in 1966 and 1967, the ever-expanding La Leche League took them over. The partitions between the offices were broken down and the resulting one large room became the home of the circulation department, headed by Marie Leonard.

But League was growing so fast that office space became overcrowded almost as quickly as it was acquired.

"We were constantly reorganizing space," Edwina said. "We would no sooner have everything all nicely organized with plenty of shelf space, and the first thing you'd know we were wall-to-wall people with boxes stacked up to the ceiling again."

"One leader visiting the office after hours remarked that the rooms were so crowded that it looked busy even when no one was there!" Marian recalled.

In 1971 the landlord, Mr. Kreiter, saw there was only one way to accommodate his space-starved tenant—he raised the roof and built a second floor onto the building. The rent was raised accordingly, to $1,280 a month.

The Executive Board was able to lay out the space and select new furnishings, and they could hardly believe their eyes when moving day came. Could it really be that those six new offices with shiny new furniture belonged to La Leche League? What a contrast to the corners of bedrooms and basements that had been League's home for so many years.

Forming The LLLI Committee

By 1971, every state, and in some cases two or three small states grouped together, had a Coordinator, so Judy Torgus and her assistants were no longer working directly with groups and leaders. Their jobs had become mainly administrative.

Also by 1971 Marybeth Doucette had a New Group Chairman in every state, so she and her assistants were no longer processing individual leader applications. They, too, were performing mainly administrative functions.

"We were climbing the same mountain, but on different sides," Judy said. "I began with people in the states (state coordinators) and later got local assistants. Marybeth began with local assistants (International New Group Chairmen) and later got New Group Chairmen within the states."

When Marybeth and Judy realized that both of their departments had evolved into primarily administrative work, they worked out a new organizational structure. Judy remained Executive Coordinator and Marybeth remained Director of New Groups, but they combined their Chicago-area assistants into the LLLI Committee.

Each LLLI Committee member was assigned several states, and she was responsible for both of

> **"We were climbing the same mountain, but on different sides."**

the state officers in her state — the State Coordinator, who was under Judy Torgus as Executive Coordinator, and the New Group Chairman, who

52

was under Marybeth Doucette as Director of New Groups. The LLLI Committee member was liaison between the states and the LLLI Executive Board.

The Committee members answered questions, received reports, solved problems, and offered advice to their state officers on a regular basis. Members of the Committee also contributed their insights and experience toward the development of various organizational procedures for LLLI.

Rosann Miller, Mary Ann Bytnar, Doris Schertz, Ruth Ann Selvey, Diane Kramer, Kay Ford, Anita Hornbostel, Karen Link, and Judy Bernetzke all served on the Committee from its inception until it was disbanded. Rita Gorski, Kathy Sklena, Dolores Minkley, Ruth Sanecki, Mary Ann Jung, Mary Welsh, Mary Ann Wiberg, Darrylyn Garrett, Jane Krueger, and Karen Bohr were part of the Committee for varying lengths of time.

The LLLI Committee functioned for about two years under both Judy and Marybeth. When Marybeth resigned early in 1972, the LLLI Executive Board asked Judy to assume full responsibility for the Committee.

It was in 1973 that the New Group Chairmen were retitled Chairman of Leader Applications (CLA).

"At one time meeting reports from new leaders were sent to the New Group Chairman for a year or so," Judy explained, "but by the early 1970s, once a leader was certified all of her reports were sent to the state coordinator. Since the New Group Chairmen were now only involved with applicants, we wanted to give them a title that would indicate what their responsibility was."

The Committee continued to function under Judy until 1976, when the department was again reorganized and the Committee disbanded.

Being Charmed By A Princess

It was like a dream come true, and the dream was fittingly brought to life by a princess — Princess Grace of Monaco.

"When we began thinking about a banquet speaker for the 1971 convention, we thought how nice it would be if we could find someone who would really give the nursing mother's morale a boost," Edwina recalled. "Nursing wasn't the 'in'

> *"She delivered a lovely message about the importance of being a mother and breastfeeding the baby."*

thing to do then like it is now, and we wanted someone who could make the mothers feel good about themselves and what they were doing."

Someone suggested Princess Grace as the banquet speaker. Back in the mid 60s, New Jersey League leader Doris Haire had sent Princess Grace a copy of THE WOMANLY ART and invited her to become an honorary member of La Leche League International, and she had responded with a most gracious acceptance.

"When Princess Grace's name was mentioned for the banquet speaker, we all said, 'Oh, no, she'd never come,'" Edwina said. "But finally Marian said, 'I don't see what we would have to lose by inviting her,' so we did."

"We asked her two years in advance, and she replied that she was very interested, but she couldn't possibly commit herself that far in advance. We wrote to her again six months before the convention, and she said she would understand if we couldn't wait and selected someone else, but she still couldn't commit herself. We all felt she was worth waiting for, and finally, three months before the convention, she wrote and said she was coming. It was really hallelujah day for us!"

Gary and Mary Kistler were co-chairmen of this convention. As expected, the crowds at the convention were record-breaking — fourteen hundred

Princess Grace of Monaco with her husband, Prince Rainier III, and their children, Caroline, Albert, and Stephanie.

mothers, eight hundred fathers, eight hundred babies and toddlers.

"Princess Grace filled the bill just beautifully," Edwina said. "She stood up there at the banquet and in her queenly way delivered a lovely message about the importance of being a mother and breastfeeding the baby."

She charmed everyone with her warmth and sincerity. "She turned out to be a lovely, motherly person," Edwina said. "We had an enormous reception for her following the banquet, and everyone there stood in line to shake her hand, and she had something to say to each and every one of them."

Besides adding glamor and excitement to the convention, Princess Grace's appearance there had far-reaching effects.

"We've been reaping the benefits ever since," Edwina said. "She made a real contribution to giving status and recognition to breastfeeding in this country."

Appointing A Public Relations Director

For some time, La Leche League's public relations consisted chiefly of letting mothers in a community where there was a League group know that if they wanted help with breastfeeding, they were welcome to come to its meetings. And probably the most frequent mention of La Leche League in newspapers today is the simple LLL series meeting notice.

But as time went on, the Board came more and more to recognize that La Leche League also had a responsibility to make the public aware of the facts (and to debunk some of the fictions!) about breastfeeding.

It was kind of ticklish, because La Leche League has always tried to avoid even the appearance of pressuring mothers to breastfeed, feeling that this was a decision each mother had to make for herself. But the Board began to realize that it was only fair to present her with information about breastfeeding that would enable her to make up her mind after hearing both sides of the baby-feeding story — the other side was already being presented persuasively by the commercial bottle-formula interests.

La Leche League mothers familiar with public relations through their own professional background or that of their husbands helped. Madge Bennett, Marilyn O'Shea, Beverly Bush Smith are names that come to mind from the early days. Beverly's series in the *Chicago Tribune*, "The Wonder

"The Board came to realize that LLL had a responsibility to make the public aware of the facts about breastfeeding."

of Watching My Baby Grow," beautifully illustrated with photographs by a *Tribune* photographer, was later published in book form. It is now out of print, but it's still a popular item in LLL group libraries lucky enough to possess a copy.

It was in 1970 that St. Louis leader Faye Young appeared at the LLLI office with proposals for handling public relations in connection with Earth Day that year. She served as publicity chairman for the 1971 convention, and before long this creative and dynamic mother became Public Relations Director for La Leche League International.

Releases emanating from the LLLI office receive Faye's particular attention. But she has always recognized the prime importance of the public relations carried on by the local groups and has offered them guidance through LEAVEN articles and

"GERALD THE THIRD is La Leche League's next 'big' publication."

through sample news releases distributed in the leader's kits. She envisions a network of Group Communicators — one for every group — and has written a Communicator's Guide, just off the press as Chapter V of the LEADER'S HANDBOOK.

Another project dear to Faye's heart, which she has been working on for several years, is a children's book in which the baby is breastfed (naturally!) *and* the other aspects of League philosophy are reflected in the doings of the small hero of the book and his family.

"By now there are a lot of children's books that show a mother nursing her baby," Faye said, "but the general attitudes in them haven't changed much. League mothers need to be able to have a book they can read to their preschoolers without reservations, with pictures the kids can enjoy and identify with. Maybe some other people who pick the book up will *see* what 'good mothering through breastfeeding' is all about."

Utterly charming in text and pictures, GERALD THE THIRD has just gone to press. It is La Leche League's next "big" publication.

Publishing A Cookbook

Any women's organization worth its salt prints up a recipe-swapping cookbook at some point. In the early 1960s Nancy Dent suggested such a project for La Leche League and started collecting recipes from League mothers.

But it was quickly realized that a La Leche League cookbook would have to be more than an exchange of recipes. The good nutrition which start with breastfeeding needs to be reinforced by good nutrition for toddlers, children, mothers (especially pregnant mothers), fathers—the whole family. So the recipes in the League cookbook had to be *nutritious*. In other words, they should exemplify the principles set forth in the nutrition chapter of THE WOMANLY ART OF BREASTFEEDING. Then they should be *tasty* (so they would get eaten) and *economical* (to suit the pocketbooks of young, growing families).

By 1965 Nancy had finished the spadework on the recipes. The project was then turned over to Roberta Johnson, who saw it through to completion. During these years it was generally referred to as "The Womanly Art of Cooking"—a title that was eventually though reluctantly relinquished because of course in League circles there is only one WOMANLY ART. Roberta obtained more recipes. She assembled a corps of testers for the recipes selected from the hundreds sent in, on the basis of the nutritious-tasty-economical criteria, so that every recipe that finally appeared in the book had been tested by at least one League mother besides the person submitting it. She found an artist, Sue Blankinship, to do the illustrations; had the recipes typed up in uniform format; laid out the pages attractively. Slowly the book took shape. Finally the money to print it was found, and in 1971 MOTHER'S IN THE KITCHEN was published and found its way into the kitchens of League mothers everywhere.

Keeping Up With The Mail

Corresponding with breastfeeding mothers in other areas quickly became a major part of the founding mothers' efforts to help women who wanted to nurse their babies. Friendships often developed between the founders and the women they helped through the mail.

"In those days, when you nursed a baby you had no one to talk to," Mary Ann Cahill explained. "It was really great when you found another nursing mother. It was instant friendship."

"Some of these women became close personal friends through correspondence," Mary White said. "We bared our souls to these mothers, and they to us, and it was beautiful."

"I remember the excitement that would be in those mothers' letters," Edwina added. "Whichever one of us they would be corresponding with was usually the only person they knew who shared any of these deep feelings we had about babies and mothering. It was so exciting when we found each other. The letters would go back and forth fast and furiously!"

But letters from other nursing mothers sometimes brought anxious moments to the founding mothers.

"Sometimes I would be so nervous when I got a letter," Edwina explained. "I'd think, 'Oh, that baby is going to be off the breast by the time she gets my letter,' so I'd phone instead. I didn't call collect because I didn't think that was right since the mother hadn't asked me to call. But I would be so nervous about that woman. The phone call always seemed to save the day."

Within the first couple of years the volume of mail got to be more than the founding mothers could handle alone, so they began looking for mothers in their groups who had the time and experience to help with the correspondence.

"Our crew of letter writers has always been terribly important and very dedicated," Edwina said. "Many of these mothers stayed up late at night after the children had gone to bed to answer letters. No two letters we received were ever alike, and they were never cut and dried. There was always so much we wanted to tell the mothers, and no two ever seemed to need exactly the same information."

The letter writers were carefully selected from among the women attending group meetings.

"As we developed groups and got to know other women who were breastfeeding mothers, we decided to call on them and see if they would be willing to help answer letters," Edwina explained. "We always asked them to take only as many letters as they felt they could comfortably handle. We knew that they had family needs to take care of first, so we encouraged them to start out low and to increase the number of letters they answered if they found they had the time."

Edwina estimated that at its peak in the mid-sixties there were forty to fifty mothers helping with the mail.

"We asked each one what she felt she would be especially good at helping another mother with—sore nipples or a fussy baby or a slow gainer," Edwina said. "We also tried to match mothering experiences. We felt a mother writing who had six children would be more comfortable corresponding with another mother who also had a large family."

Edwina handled all of the correspondence out of her home until fall of 1963 when letters were sent out to the volunteer letter writers from the LLLI office.

In the mid sixties Mary Ann Cahill took charge of the letter writers.

"There was so much mail that we felt it needed its own little department," Mary Ann explained. "We needed one person to be responsible for keeping in touch with the letter writers to see that they had the information they needed to answer mothers' questions. They needed lots of encouragement because it was such a big job, and we felt it was important to be sure someone was letting them know how much we appreciated the tremendous job they were doing."

During the late sixties and early seventies League grew at an astonishing rate, and the letters requesting help decreased proportionately.

"As League grew and we got more and more groups, the letter writing decreased because mothers were able to get help in their own area," Mary Ann explained. "When we did get letters asking for breastfeeding help, we could usually just write a brief note, enclose a few reprints, and give the mother the name and phone number of a leader in her area. So the volume of letters that had to be personally answered decreased substantially."

The staff of letter writers is once again being handled out of the LLLI office. Annamae Boutin took over in 1976 and coordinates both the distribution of the mail and the letter writers themselves.

"Letter writers are unsung in many ways," Mary Ann said, "but heroes to the mothers who are alone in breastfeeding their babies and find encouragement and hope and LLLove in a white and blue envelope. Their number is small, about thirty, but their spirit is mighty and extends as far as the mails carry."

Expanding The Professional Advisory Board

Although the heart of La Leche League is mother-to-mother help, the founders recognized from the beginning that they needed professional support.

Fate provided them with two doctors—Dr. White and Dr. Ratner—from the beginning. The founders relied heavily on these good doctors in the early days of the League, calling on them for both moral support and medical information pertaining to breastfeeding. The Medical Advisory Board was born.

It wasn't long before the founders began hearing about other doctors who were particularly supportive of breastfeeding.

"We felt we needed support from the medical community," Mary White said, "to let people know there were doctors who supported breastfeeding and our efforts to help nursing mothers."

"There were so few doctors who were pro-breastfeeding that we felt we should have those who did support breastfeeding working with us," Edwina said. "We wanted to be able to draw on their knowledge and experience."

The first to join Dr. White and Dr. Ratner as a medical advisor to the League was Dr. E. Robbins Kimball, who practiced pediatrics in Evanston, headed the Evanston Milk Bank, and was one of the few doctors who had a large percentage of nursing mothers in his practice.

"We invited him to come and talk to our Board meeting in 1958," Edwina recalled. "He was so enthusiastic about breastfeeding, and we were really taken with him."

Soon after, Marian heard Dr. Robert Mendelsohn give a talk, "Whom Is the Hospital For?" She knew at once that here was a kindred soul and invited him to the next Medical Advisors meeting.

Other doctors followed in quick succession—Dr. Carolyn Rawlins, the first obstetrician on the Board, Drs. Frank Richardson and Herman Meyer, both of whom had written books particularly supportive of breastfeeding.

Many of the doctors now on the Board, such as Dr. James Good, Dr. Paul Busam, Dr. Richard Applebaum, Dr. Hugh Riordan, Dr. R. L. Goedecke, and Dr. Mark Thoman, became members of the Board through their breastfeeding wives.

During the late sixties, the Board began looking for doctors who had a special expertise to offer—jaundice, immunology, allergies, emotional needs, natural childbirth.

In 1971 the Medical Advisory Board became the Professional Advisory Board. It was felt that this was a more accurate title, since not all of the members were M.D.s.

"We consult Board members about individual cases, ask them to read and approve any medical information we publish, and seek their opinions on published information about breastfeeding that comes to our attention," Edwina said.

"Seven mothers would only have been seven mothers without the doctors," Marian said. "They provided us with information and answers we needed, and gave us credibility and acceptability in the medical community."

The Printed Words Flow On

During these middle years LA LECHE LEAGUE NEWS continued to flourish. Under the two-year editorship of Florence Carlson it grew to twelve pages, looking more professional all the time. In 1964 Rosemary Fahey became editor; Lea Murphy, who had assisted Florence, continued to help with the art work, and her charming drawings graced the pages of NEWS from time to time for a number of years.

It was during this period that the first area Inserts began to make their appearance in NEWS. As the League population in a state or area became large enough to warrant it, a special Insert containing LLL news of local interest was prepared there and sent in to Franklin Park to be bound with the copies of the NEWS going to subscribers in that area. When Rosemary became editor, there were already eight of these Inserts, and the number continued to increase through the years until eventually every copy of the NEWS mailed out had one. (For the record, Utah was the last state to come into the Insertfold, in 1976.)

NEWS circulation continued to grow during the 60s, reaching nearly 5,000 by the time Rosemary took the editorial helm. Mailing it began to be more of an undertaking than in the days when both editorial and circulation work was done on the Tompson dining room table. A League family, the Mortensens of Franklin Park, in 1960 relieved the Tompsons of the mailing chores, and six of the nine Mortensens labored mightily bimonthly to get the NEWS properly addressed and to the post office. Dolores Mortensen remembers the rejoicing when a secondhand hand-cranked addressing machine was purchased and the subscription list was transferred to stencils. But the list continued to expand; the Mortensen children began to grow up and become gainfully employed elsewhere; and when LLLI moved to its new office on Minneapolis Avenue in 1965, the stencils migrated from the Mortensens' basement to proper Circulation Department quarters at LLLI, joined en route by a grander (but still secondhand) *foot-operated* addressing machine. At about this time Marie Leonard took over the handling of subscriptions—and the mailings were right back in the laps of the Tompson family, who for the next four years, with occasional assists from other League families, got the NEWS out over the weekend after it was delivered to the office by printer John Hudtez.

Back to editorial matters. The NEWS got longer— sixteen pages — and still more attractive. But, as had happened with Florence, Rosemary's growing family began to cut down on the amount of time she could devote to it. In 1966 she was given an assistant—Mary Carson, who following the publication of the 1963 edition of THE WOMANLY ART

NEWS editorial board — Mary White, Mary Carson, Edwina, and Betty.

had been standing in the wings ready and willing to help with any editorial work LLLI might need. But this was only a stop-gap measure, and a year later Rosemary turned over the editorial chair (and Mary Carson) to Board member Nell Ryan.

Nell had served as chairman of the first LLLI Convention in 1964 and then as Illinois Coordinator, so she brought to her new assignment an intimate acquaintance with the League organization as well as the imagination, zest, and creativity of a good editor.

"The tone of NEWS changes with new editors," Marian said. "Every editor gives a flavor of her own. When I was editing it I was still in my twenties and still having babies, and everything was very immediate. The things that appealed to me and the things I felt should go in were very different, for instance, from the things I'm writing about now in my NEWS column, Memos from Marian."

Nell began editing LEAVEN as well as NEWS in 1968, and carried on as editor of both LLL periodicals until 1970. She made several innovations in NEWS, including a January/February Insert Issue, containing a potpourri of items gleaned from the Inserts, and a May/June Father's Issue with articles chiefly for and about fathers. And every issue sparkled with her own particular editorial touch. Who can forget the picture of the Ryans' five sons, captioned BOY, O BOY, O BOY, O BOY, O BOY, O —followed by a picture of newborn Marynel ending the series with a triumphant GIRL!

In 1970 Nell retired to begin work on her doctorate in psychology. The oldest Tompson daughter, Melanie, stepped into the breach with competence and aplomb until Mary Carson came into the League office on a permanent basis as editor of NEWS and other LLLI publications in 1971. By that time the circulation of NEWS was over 22,000.

Meanwhile, information sheets, booklets, flyers continued to multiply. Outstanding during this period was the picture booklet BREASTFEEDING YOUR BABY, prepared by Judy Good, with drawings by Joy Sidor. The text accompanying the pictures presented the breastfeeding story in short, simple words. Another short pamphlet, WHEN YOU BREASTFEED YOUR BABY, subtitled "Helpful Hints for the Early Weeks," was prepared for use especially in hospitals; and the hospital nurse was given a complementary assist with HOW THE NURSE CAN HELP THE BREASTFEEDING MOTHER.

The revised edition of THE WOMANLY ART OF BREASTFEEDING went through thirteen printings; by 1971, 50,000 were being printed at a time—a far cry from the first tentative thousand of the looseleaf edition. The new MOTHER'S IN THE KITCHEN went through three printings during its first year, 1971.

Continuing to Answer the Need for Breastfeeding Help

In 1964, when Edwina's other League duties began taking too much of her time for her to handle the phone calls for breastfeeding help, the League phone was taken over by Dale Simpson, who kept it for about a year.

It then passed to Ruth Sanecki, who knows exactly how long she had it — "three years, ten months and seventeen days!"

"Some calls were cut and dry," Ruth said, "and some required extensive help. Some mothers just needed someone to talk to, not about breastfeeding problems but about mothering problems. There are several children walking around today that I feel I helped raise, from coming home from the hospital to the first tooth to the first step!

"My children were small when I had the League phone," Ruth said, "and I know at the time they thought that their mother had just come equipped with a phone hanging out of her ear. You would be surprised what I learned to do with one hand while I was talking on the phone."

About 1966 a second League phone was installed in Gerry Kilcoyne's home. By 1968 Ruth and Gerry were each averaging about twenty calls a week. But by that time the League groups in many large cities were getting their own phones and being listed in the telephone directory, so many calls began going to them.

In the late 1960s the LLLI office began taking calls for breastfeeding help during office hours and leaving a recorded message with a local leader's phone number after the office was closed.

A League leader, Harriet Modrich, was brought in to handle these calls to the office, and later another leader, Annamae Boutin, who had come to work at the office, began taking some of them. Even so, when it happens that both Harriet and Annamae are busy with other calls, an occasional call gets routed to Edwina, just as in the old days. Marybeth Doucette also handles many of these calls, and Marian, Judy Torgus, and Betty Wagner occasionally take calls, and so do Mary Ann Cahill and Vi Lennon when they are in the office.

For no matter what other pressing business needs tending to, a mother's call for breastfeeding help still gets priority at International, just as it does at every level of League.

Founding mothers in front of the office, displaying their caricatures made from bowling pins made for them by a Colorado leader — Marian, Mary Ann Cahill, Edwina, Vi, Betty (also holding Mary Ann Kerwin's doll), and Mary White.

Marian presenting Dr. Paul György with a plaque commemorating the establishment of the Paul György Award. Dr. Herbert Ratner looks on.

La Leche League Comes of Age

"Little Leaguers" populate all LLL gatherings.

59

La Leche League
...Recognizes The Need For A New Governing Structure

It was the enormous growth of La Leche League that necessitated changing the Executive Board to the Board of Directors in 1972.

From the time the Board became the Executive Board in 1962, its function had been to handle both the structural part of the organization and all matters pertaining to League policy and philosophy.

By the mid 1960s the Executive Board began delegating authority to various members of the Board, putting them in charge of different aspects of the League's organization. This cut down on the amount of work that had to be accomplished at Board meetings, yet allowed all the authority for running the organization to remain with the Board. Board members who were responsible for certain aspects of the League's organization were directly responsible to the entire Executive Board.

But by 1972 La Leche League had become so large that the Executive Board had to meet weekly — sometimes oftener — to make all the necessary decisions.

"It became impossible for the Executive Board to meet often enough to make all of the day-to-day decisions involved in running the League," Edwina explained. "That was when Garrett Gruner, the husband of a League leader, met with us. He was a business management consultant, and he offered to talk to us about the possibility of a change that would make us more efficient."

Garrett analyzed the League's situation and offered a solution to it.

"He agreed that the League was far too big for the day-to-day decisions to be made by the Executive Board as a team. The fact that no decisions could be made until we all got together would be bound to cause delays when the Board couldn't get together for a meeting.

"Then he talked to us about how a Board of Directors functions," Edwina said. "He said that the Board of Directors should be the governing body with an administrator to administer the Board's decisions. He said our organization had too many departments and too many facets for the Board as a whole to be in charge of them. He told us that the Board should stop spending its time making the day-to-day decisions and instead spend its time and energy making the organization's policies. The procedures for implementing these policies would be put into effect by the various department heads, all of whom would be directly responsible to the Board of Directors.

"This was a totally new concept for us," Edwina recalled. "We thought it sounded much better than the way we had been doing things. We were delighted at the thought of being able to cut out those weekly Board meetings!"

So in October of 1972 the Executive Board became the Board of Directors, strictly a policy-making body. The day-to-day decisions were put in the hands of the Administrator, who by unanimous agreement of the Board was Betty Wagner. Far from meeting weekly, the Board of Directors set their meetings at just four a year.

The Board of Directors with an Administrator provided an efficient method of handling La Leche League's affairs. It would have been incomprehensible to the founding mothers in 1956 that their desire to help a few friends nurse their babies would someday result in a complex organizational structure governing a worldwide network of groups and leaders.

...Clarifies Its Philosophy

No one was more surprised by La Leche League's phenomenal growth than the founding mothers themselves. Because they never envisioned the extensive network of groups and leaders that developed, they did not have a plan for coping with the needs of a large organization. It was always a case of catching up with rather than anticipating the needs that developed as the League expanded and grew. The need to clearly define La Leche League philosophy was one of the needs that evolved as the organization spread across the country.

In the early 1960s when the founding mothers first saw the need to certify La Leche League representatives, all potential leaders were certified through just one person. Mary Jane Brizzolara, working closely with the founding mothers, presented League philosophy to all of the women who asked to become leaders.

As more women applied for leadership and the job became too big for one person to handle, several Chicago-based New Group Chairmen began handling applications and interpreting League philosophy to leader-applicants. As the number of applicants continued to grow through the late sixties, state-level New Group Chairmen were appointed to handle applications, and it became their job to interpret League philosophy to the applicants in their states.

It was in the early 1970s that some members of

the LLLI Committee noticed that there was variation from one state to another in the way League philosophy was interpreted and presented. Since it was not spelled out anyplace, everyone seemed to have her own idea about exactly what constituted League philosophy.

"We saw that an applicant could become easily certified in one state, but not in another," LLLI Committee member Mary Ann Bytnar explained. "The New Group Chairman in each state was presenting League philosophy to the applicants based on her own interpretation of exactly what League philosophy was. Each New Group Chairman had a slightly different idea about the philosophy an applicant had to agree with in order to become a leader."

Because they were concerned about the variety of interpretations of League philosophy, Mary Ann Bytnar, Rita Gorsky, and Rosann Miller, all members of the LLLI Committee, asked the LLLI Executive Board for permission to try to clarify and define League philosophy.

In early 1972 the Board gave the go-ahead, and the three women began working to develop the Guidelines to League Philosophy. They met almost weekly over a period of a year and a half to define exactly what constituted League philosophy.

Because the League manual, THE WOMANLY ART OF BREASTFEEDING, was the official source of League policy and philosophy, the women used it as the basis for their work.

"We took the manual and pulled it apart," Mary Ann explained. "We categorized all of the philosophy in it. We kept narrowing it down and narrowing it down, and finally we got it down to eight categories."

Mary Ann, Rosann, and Rita presented the Board with a paragraph describing each of the eight concepts, and the Board then condensed each paragraph into one sentence. In September of 1972 the eight concepts were officially adopted. A ninth concept on the baby's need for constant mothering was added in the fall of 1973, and a tenth concept on discipline in the fall of 1975.

The concepts clarified for everyone — leaders, applicants, and New Group Chairmen — exactly what constituted League philosophy. The concepts provided every mother who applied for leadership, no matter where she lived, with a clear understanding of the League philosophy she would be expected to represent as a La Leche League leader. The adoption of the concepts brought uniformity to the requirements for League leadership.

WE IN LLL BELIEVE

1. Mothering through breastfeeding is the most natural and effective way of understanding and satisfying the needs of the baby.
2. Mother and baby need to be together early and often to establish a satisfying relationship and an adequate milk supply.
3. The baby has a basic need for his mother's love and presence which is as intense as his need for food. This need remains even though his mother may be absent for a period of time for needs or reasons of her own.
4. Breast milk is the superior infant food.
5. For the healthy, full-term baby breast milk is the only food necessary until baby shows signs of needing solids, about the middle of the first year after birth.
6. Ideally the breastfeeding relationship will continue until the baby outgrows the need.
7. Alert and active participation by the mother in childbirth is a help in getting breastfeeding off to a good start.
8. The father's role in the breastfeeding relationship is one of provider, protector, helpmate, and companion to the mother; by thus supporting her he enables her to mother the baby more completely.
9. Good nutrition means eating a well-balanced and varied diet of foods in as close to their natural state as possible.
10. Ideally, discipline is based on loving guidance.

...Develops A Human Relations Training Program

The seeds for La Leche League's Human Relations Training program were sown in the early 1970s as Granville Sydnor listened to his leader-wife counsel breastfeeding mothers. After observing Jackie and other leaders work with mothers, Granville became convinced that League leaders could benefit from a greater knowledge of how to listen and respond with empathy to mothers' feelings.

"Granville observed that leaders were usually much too ready to give advice and information without first listening to the mother's feelings," Edwina explained. "He felt that a basic ingredient in helping people was learning to listen to their feelings. If you immediately moved in with advice, it might not be the advice the mother needed because you hadn't listened long enough to see what her real needs were."

LLLI Committee member Kay Ford knew Jackie Sydnor, who was Louisiana's New Group Chairman, and was very interested in the Sydnors' proposal to develop a human relations training program for the League. Kay arranged for Edwina to meet Jackie and Granville at the 1971 Louisiana state meeting.

"I became convinced that the Sydnors had something to offer that LLL could use," Edwina said. "It was obvious to us that leaders wanted this kind of help. More and more, state meetings were offering programs on helping techniques, and we had no way of controlling the content or quality of these programs. So we decided it would be a good idea to have a program of our own."

Granville flew to Franklin Park early in 1972 and

ran a two-day workshop in which most Board members participated. At the conclusion of the workshop, the Board accepted the Sydnors' proposal to develop a human relations training program specifically for League.

Granville suggested that Diane Kramer be appointed director of the program, and the Board agreed.

Jackie and Granville, along with Nadine Parkhill, agreed to adapt a training manual specifically for League, using League terms and examples. They worked with many League leaders and Executive Board members while preparing the book to ensure that the examples used were as representative as possible.

The HRT workbook was published late in 1972. HRT trainers were selected and trained, and the La Leche League HRT program was in full swing. The trainers hold HRT verbal sessions for small groups of interested leaders who have completed the ninety-nine page workbook. During the verbal sessions, the leaders have an opportunity to sharpen and put into practice the skills they learned in the workbook.

"The program has been very popular among leaders who have completed it," Diane said. "It has provided them with a more broadly based, empathetic way of relating to people, and has often helped them to become more understanding wives and mothers as well as better League leaders."

...Initiates Information Service Centers

It was the desire to extend La Leche League's help into areas where League groups did not or could not exist that inspired Diane Kramer to initiate the LLLI Information Service Centers in 1972.

"The LLLI Committee was in touch with people who badly needed what we had to offer but who just couldn't have a program of leadership," Diane explained. "We wanted there to be some way these people could be in touch with us so that the help they were giving mothers would be our help."

She suggested that League devise an entirely different set-up to serve mothers in areas where the mothers were not in a position to become leaders or where it would be impractical for a League group to exist.

"We knew we wouldn't be certifying leaders in these situations. We weren't going to be able to be on hand to see that everything was going to function the way it should and that they were following our policies. We didn't want to lend them our name as such because we couldn't be on hand to supervise. So we had to devise an arrangement by which they could receive and distribute our information, even though they could not become leaders and would not be holding series meetings," Diane explained.

The Board adopted Diane's suggestion and named Eleanor Randall Information Service Director.

"An individual, an institution, or a group of people can become an Information Center," Eleanor explained. "The individuals who act as Information Centers are about as varied a group as you can possibly get. We have missionaries, wives of doctors who help in clinics, medical students, doctors, and nuns, to name a few."

Since the first Information Service Center was formed in Mendoza in September of 1973, there have been a total of sixty-one Centers. Forty-four Centers are currently active, ten of them in the United States.

"The Centers can operate in the United States in areas that do not have active leaders who can serve them," Eleanor explained.

Several of the Information Centers in the United States are located in urban areas. The Kentucky Frontier Nursing Service is also a subscriber. Although they are not League leaders, the nurses are thus able to provide LLL information to the women they serve. A government library subscribes for reference purposes.

"Drs. Michael and Niles Newton's son is a subscriber," Eleanor said. "He is a medical student at Harvard and works in a clinic. He felt the breastfeeding help there wasn't very good, so the Newtons subscribed to the Information Service for him so that he can provide our information to the mothers in the clinic."

The fee to subscribe to the Information Service is $12.00 for the first year and $8.00 for each succeeding year. A higher rate is charged for the first year to cover the cost of the initial packet each new subscriber is given. This includes a copy of THE WOMANLY ART OF BREASTFEEDING, a copy of nearly every reprint and information sheet, and a subscription to the NEWS and LEAVEN. Information Service subscribers are automatically sent a copy of every new or revised information sheet or reprint.

"We send it to them without asking them to write and request it after it is announced in LEAVEN because we want to keep them as up to date as possible," Eleanor explained.

Subscribers to the Information Service are free to write to LLLI and ask any questions or get help with any breastfeeding situations that they might encounter. They enjoy referral service to members of the Professional Advisory Board and have access to all of the information that La Leche League has.

"Subscribers have some of the privileges of a

leader," Edwina explained, "but they cannot speak for LLL as a leader can. They are not official representatives of La Leche League as leaders are."

"The number of Service Centers has grown tremendously, and we expect it to grow even more," Eleanor said.

The development of the LLLI Information Service Centers was just one more step toward La Leche League's goal of providing help for any woman, anywhere, who wants to nurse her baby.

...Holds Physicians Seminars

Getting good breastfeeding information to physicians has always been one of La Leche League's goals. But getting the League's breastfeeding information into physicians' hands was primarily dependent on an individual League mother sharing either her personal experience or the League's written material with her own doctor.

In 1971 Vera Turton came up with a far more efficient approach to sharing La Leche League's information with physicians.

"She knew that sometimes physicians got credit for going to meetings," Marian recalled. "It was her idea to see if we could put on a program for doctors and get it accredited. We found out that the AMA wouldn't accredit us in advance, but they said that if we wanted to put on a seminar for physicians they would come out and survey us to see if we could be accredited."

So Marian set up a program committee which included Drs. Niles Newton, Ratner, White and Mendelsohn.

"The doctors contributed what they thought doctors needed to hear about breastfeeding, and I contributed what I thought they needed to hear from the mothers' point of view," Marian explained.

The first Physicians' Breastfeeding Seminar became a reality in 1973. It was attended by only a handful of doctors, twenty or thirty, Marian recalled. But it received a gratifying compliment from one of the doctors who was surveying it for the AMA.

"He told us, 'Even if you aren't accredited, please continue giving these seminars because there is noplace else for doctors to get this kind of information,'" Marian recalled.

"I really didn't think we were going to get accredited," Marian said. "After so many years of being outside the establishment, I just couldn't believe that they would accept us."

But accreditation was granted.

"The AMA gave us what they call provisional accreditation," Marian explained. "We were accredited for the next couple of years, and then they said they would resurvey us to see whether we should be given permanent accreditation. It was provisional because of our small budget — they were concerned that we might not be able to continue to present yearly seminars on such a small amount of money. They are resurveying us this year and will make the decision whether or not to grant permanent accreditation."

In addition to the AMA, the American College of Obstetricians and Gynecologists and the American Academy of Family Physicians have also accredited the yearly seminars. Every one since the first has had a capacity audience. Sue Peaster, then Carol Kolar, have coordinated them.

"We have between one hundred and one hundred and twenty-five doctors attend every year," Marian said. "These seminars are specifically designed for physicians. We work with nurses mainly on the state and local levels."

Evaluation forms are sent to physicians who attend the seminars so that the League can gauge the effectiveness of its presentation.

"We send the evaluation forms out about three months after the seminar so that it gives the doctor time to see how the information is working," Marian explained. "Invariably we get a large percentage of the forms back, which in itself is a good sign. Most of the forms have very good comments. In one hospital they changed the whole nursery set-up as a result of the information they got at the seminar. The babies were allowed to nurse immediately after delivery and given to the mothers thereafter on demand. They said now the mothers' milk was coming in much faster, and engorgement was no longer a problem.

"We've also heard from mothers whose doctor has come to a seminar, and they say that the doctor has changed his entire practice. One doctor in Michigan hired La Leche League leaders as breastfeeding counselors. He has done a chart showing how the incidence of problems has dropped since he has been providing this kind of care for his mothers."

The seminar held on the eve of the Fifth International Convention in 1974 was the occasion for the announcement by LLLI of the Paul György Annual Awards for the best original papers on breastfeeding submitted by students enrolled in medical schools. They were named to honor a long-time friend and supporter of La Leche League for his distinguished contributions to human milk research. Dr. György served as one of the judges of the first group of papers in 1975; he died February 29, 1976. These awards, encouraging medical research in breastfeeding, serve as another link between La Leche League and the medical community.

The seminars have all been moderated by Dr. Ratner.

"He really has a gift for moderating," Marian said, "plus he has such a broad knowledge of what's going on in infant feeding and knows how to relate it philosophically with life in this world.

"These seminars have tremendous potential. We have been asked to hold them more often than once a year, but for now, one a year is what we can arrange."

...Fills The Need For A Teaching Film

Over the years the founding mothers have found themselves thrust into any number of situations they never expected to be in and wouldn't have been in except for their decision back in 1956 to help a few friends nurse their babies.

Marian recalled the sense of disbelief and amazement she has felt on so many occasions.

"So many times I have found myself saying, 'Am I really here? Is this really happening to me just because I breastfed my babies?'"

These feelings were probably never stronger than when Marian found herself in movie star Natalie Wood's home in 1973 when the League's teaching film, *Mother and Child*, was being made.

The project had begun, as so many LLL projects have, as the brainchild of a League couple.

"I was in North Carolina for a state meeting, and Wilma Asrael, the state coordinator, told me she would like for me to meet a League father who was interested in doing a film on breastfeeding for the League," Marian recalled. "He told me that his wife had been helped by La Leche League, and he would like to do something for the League. He said he would make the film, print it, and send it out free of charge to anyone who wanted to show it. It sounded like an incredible deal."

Financing for the film was kicked off by Denver LLLers, and followed by LLLers in Zion, Illinois, and other scattered groups across the country. But it requires an enormous amount of money to make a film, and it was slow going.

"Then California League leader Pat Brewster interested Mr. Cattani of the Mary Jane Company in contributing to the film," Marian said. "He started out offering $1,000 and in the end contributed $30,000." That was eighty percent of the amount needed, and when combined with the money the League had already collected, there was enough money for *Mother and Child* to become a reality.

More good luck soon followed.

"Someone in Hollywood told us that Natalie Wood had been helped by the League and would be willing to donate her services for the film," Marian said. "Then we got the same kind of news about Susan Saint James—she was successfully nursing her daughter Sunshine with the help of a League group and would like to do whatever she could to help us in return."

So with the script, $38,000, and two movie stars, shooting got under way.

Most of the film takes place in a hospital, where nurses are shown helping a new mother get started with breastfeeding her baby.

"It's an actual new mother with her baby, so she reacts pretty much as a new mother really would," Marian said.

The part of the film in which Natalie Wood appears was shot at the star's home.

"I remember sitting in her family room waiting for her to come downstairs," Marian said, "and saying to myself, 'Am I really here? Am I really sitting in Natalie Wood and Robert Wagner's family room?'"

When Natalie Wood asked that her lines be put on cue cards, Marian got the job of writing out the script on the cards.

"I was on my hands and knees writing out the whole script. Their children were around me telling me about everything going on in the family, just like children everyplace. I heard Robert Wagner's voice as he came in the front door, but then he left again. I said to myself, 'Oh, no. Here I was being so good and writing out the script and now I've missed getting to see Robert Wagner.'"

The filming began, and Marian found herself with another job.

"It was my job to be the cue card holder. That is an art," Marian explained. "I had these big cards, and as she finished reading from one, I had to drop it without dropping the others. And you can't make any noise as you're dropping them because it will get on the sound track."

Marian recalled that she nearly lost both the cards and her composure when Robert Wagner unexpectedly came back into the house and walked into the room.

"Bob Wagner came in and helped me hold the cue cards. Again I found I was saying to myself, 'This can't be real—I'm not really here in Natalie Wood's house with Bob Wagner helping me hold cue cards.'"

As had been promised, the film was printed and made available on loan free of charge to any group wishing to show it.

"The film is intended as a modeling role for nurses," Marian explained. "There are very few films for nurses that give them suggestions on how to deal with a nursing mother."

La Leche League groups are using it, Marian said. It has been shown all over the country on television, and it has been purchased by several schools of nursing.

...Establishes A Liaison With The Medical Community

From the beginning, La Leche League was greeted enthusiastically by mothers who so desperately wanted the help the League offered, but the medical community was not quite so receptive. Many doctors felt that breastfeeding fell into the medical domain, and that one nursing mother was not qualified to advise another.

"I don't blame the doctors for not being quick to leap at us with open arms," Marian explained. "They were used to getting their information from scientific sources, not mothers. And our suggestions were so different from the little available textbook information about breastfeeding that they were suspicious of us."

But as time passed, doctors began to see and value what La Leche League had to offer. In 1973 the League began formally and officially to work toward improving relations with the medical community. It was then that the physicians' seminars were initiated.

That same year Betty Ann Countryman requested Board approval for a Professional Liaison Department. Her goal was to work toward establishing better communication, greater understanding, and mutual respect between La Leche League and the medical community.

"La Leche League has so much to offer doctors and their patients," Betty Ann said. "The development of a mutually respectful and understanding attitude would bring many advantages to La Leche League and the medical community—and most of all, to the nursing couple."

As a registered nurse, wife of a Professional Advisory Board member, and member of the LLI Board of Directors, Betty Ann hoped to help bridge the existing gap. She began by looking for state level representatives for the new Professional Liaison Department.

"Most, but not all, are nurses," Betty Ann said. "Those who are not, almost without exception, have a specific tie-in some way with the medical community."

These state-level representatives became known as Area Professional Liaison leaders (APLs). The APL's primary responsibilities outside the League include fostering good professional public relations, speaking to professional groups, and providing the medical community with League information on breastfeeding and related subjects. Within the League, APLs explain and interpret professional attitudes and language to League leaders and mothers. They help leaders help mothers learn to dialogue with their doctors.

APLs also handle questions of a medical nature, either providing answers based on the recommendations of the League's Professional Advisory Board or referring LLL leaders and mothers directly to the PAB for help.

"But I think one of the most important things we do," Betty Ann said, "is to help LLL leaders and mothers everywhere understand their rights and responsibilities both as mothers and as patients."

...Develops Research Guidelines

As La Leche League grew and the number of nursing mothers grew, the interest in doing research on human milk grew, also.

"Researchers began to realize that La Leche League mothers were an excellent source of human milk," Edwina said. "They began getting in touch with League people in their area and asking them to contribute milk.

"Some of it was worthwhile research, and some of it wasn't. The League leaders weren't ordinarily in a position to make that distinction. In the cases where it wasn't worthwhile research, the leaders were being taken advantage of.

"Even in the cases where the research was bona fide, leaders were still sometimes taken advantage of. A researcher might get an enthusiastic leader to do a lot of his work for him. She would be running around doing all of his collecting and phoning and corresponding and never even get paid. But she thought she was supposed to do it," Edwina explained. "Because the request came from the medical community, some leaders were misled into thinking that we would expect them to cooperate."

It was the prevalence of such situations that made the Board realize the necessity of setting up some guidelines for League groups' participation in research projects. The program operated informally for several years and in 1974 officially became the Research Department.

"We sent a copy of the guidelines out to all our leaders," Edwina said, "and we said that they could not participate in any research in the name of La Leche League unless the project was first cleared by our office. We explained that we were requiring this on the advice of our Professional Advisory Board and that it was to protect both them and the mothers.

"We now require of the researcher that he submit a proper protocol that tells us who is doing the research, where the money to finance it is coming from, and what individual or institution is sponsoring it. We also want to know exactly how he plans to use the League mothers, and of course we want to know the purpose of the research and what he expects to do with the results. All this information is put into the protocol."

In cases where the purpose of the research is simple and obvious and the amount of milk required is very small, approval may be granted fairly quickly. "If we have no questions at all in our minds about it, Marian and I will present it to Dr. Ratner, and then it is cleared." Edwina explained.

But most of the research projects are much more complicated, and they are sent around to the entire committee, which consists of several members of the Professional Advisory Board and Board of Directors.

The committee is first and foremost concerned as to whether what is required will in any way be a risk to mother or baby, or come between them at all. The other matters covered in the protocol are also given due attention.

If the committee has any questions about research which looks as if it will probably be approved, these questions are sent back to the researcher to be answered. His reply is sent out to the committee, and then all of the comments received from the committee have to be sent out to each committee member before a decision can be made.

"All of that means that one person, and that person was me for quite a while," Edwina said, "has to spend a lot of time reading all of this material, summarizing it — some protocols are twenty and thirty pages long — sending it around to the committee, getting the responses, and keeping track of it all. When it got to be too much for me, we turned it over to our reference librarian, Carolyn Hayes."

It soon became apparent that Carolyn was spending an enormous amount of time handling all of the research requests.

"In 1975 we finally said that we just couldn't afford to lose that much of a staff member's time, plus the mounting cost of postage, duplicating material, and so on," Edwina said. "We decided that the researchers would have to share this burden. We asked the members of our Professional Advisory Board, and they agreed that it would be quite appropriate to charge for our service. They are the ones who set the fee—$50.00; $15.00 for students.

"Every once in a while a League leader writes and says she is so embarrassed," Edwina said. "She has talked to a doctor who has approached her about doing research, and she was all agog and said she would write for permission. Then she finds out that we require the doctor to pay a $50.00 fee, and she is incensed that we could do such a crass thing. I've had to write many letters to leaders explaining why the fee is necessary."

Research projects are occasionally turned down by the committee, for a variety of reasons.

"Sometimes it is the way in which they want to use the mothers," Edwina said. "They might want to put her in the hospital for two or three days and separate her from her baby.

"Sometimes they want to give the baby some other kind of food or formula. Or they may want to inject the mother or the baby, and we won't have any part of that. Or the project may require too much of the mother's time and work a hardship on her that way.

"One doctor wanted to give iron to the babies," Edwina said, "and we said, 'No.' The researcher said, 'I'm going to be using a control group, and I can arrange it so that the babies who will be getting the iron won't be the League mothers' babies, they'll be the other babies.' We believe that iron given directly to the baby may be harmful, so we told him that we didn't want to be part of a research project that would necessitate giving iron to any babies, League or otherwise, because we believe it to be risky."

Edwina said that research projects are sometimes turned down because the purpose of the research is cloudy. "It may not be clear exactly what they are trying to do or what they expect to do with it after they find it."

But of the approximately one hundred research requests that are received by LLLI every year, Carolyn Hayes estimated that eighty to ninety are approved. Scientists as well as mothers are rediscovering the wonders of human milk.

...Convenes In Chicago

Guest speakers galore delighted the twenty-five hundred adults who attended the 1974 convention at the Palmer House in Chicago (and were politely endured by the fifteen hundred babies and small children who provided what some felt was a rather charming obbligato to their remarks).

Hope Melnick was chairman for this convention, with the able assistance of Bill Stiles.

The keynote address, delivered by international authority Derrick B. Jelliffe, was titled "Human Milk — A Unique Gift of Love, A Natural World Resource." Dr. Jelliffe told the audience, "Every day malnutrition in the world's poorer countries kills and damages more children than all the man-made and natural catastrophes combined. Human milk contains over one hundred different constituents identified to date; more will undoubtedly be discovered. While it may be possible to bring up young on the milk of other species, it is quite impossible to humanize cow's milk."

Dr. Niles Newton, whose involvement with the League dated back to 1959, delivered the banquet speech, "Take Your Baby With You."

"She is a professional woman who is also the epitome of motherhood," Edwina said. "As a psychologist she understands the importance of the need for mother and baby to be together. When her

Susan Saint James was a special guest speaker at the 1974 convention.

four children were small, she followed her profession only to the extent that it didn't interfere with her mothering. Though she is well recognized in her field, she is always first and foremost a mother. She is proud of being a mother and all that it entails, and it is always a thrill to have her share those feelings with us."

A special guest speaker at the banquet was actress Susan Saint James.

"California League leader Kittie Frantz wrote and told us that Susan was in her group," Edwina said. "She thought the League was tremendous and was very appreciative of all that League had done for her. When we invited Susan to be our guest speaker at the banquet she was delighted and very pleased to be invited. She was tremendously popular with the young mothers at the convention."

Dr. Lee Salk, author of *How To Raise a Human Being* and a number of other wise best-selling books on child care, assured the mothers that their instinct to reach for the baby and cuddle it when it cries is a sound one. "People nowadays are showing more interest in being good parents, and that is a good thing," he said, "because the future of our civilization depends on our children. It is up to parents to provide their children with the kind of nurture that will enable them to become trustworthy, socially responsible, compassionate human beings."

Other VIPs at the convention were Karen Pryor, who wrote *Nursing Your Baby*; Dana Raphael, author of *The Tender Gift – Breastfeeding*; English author Sheila Kitzinger (*The Experience of Childbirth*); Niles Newton (*The Family Book of Child Care*), and, of course, our beloved Charlotte Aiken of the *Child-Family Digest*, the League's earliest guiding light.

It was with the 1974 convention that Hope Melnick was named LLLI Conference Director.

"Hope had served on a committee for the 1971 convention," Edwina recalled. "When everyone else was still thinking about what to do, Hope had her job completely done. Naturally you notice someone like that, and Betty and I made a mental note."

Following the 1971 convention, the Board decided to appoint a permanent conference director, and Hope was the obvious choice for the post.

"We decided that it would make sense to put one person in charge of conventions and have the local chairmen work with her," Edwina said. "We had always been starting from scratch with each convention as the new chairmen learned the ropes. With a permanent Conference Director, we wouldn't have that problem. We felt that if Hope would be willing, she could do an outstanding job."

Hope enthusiastically accepted the position of LLLI Conference Director.

"Hope is a person who believes that you've got to make a contribution in this world," Edwina said. "She gives so generously of her time and talent to do an outstanding job. She is beautifully organized and has made a name for herself in the hotel world. Now we can hardly remember how we got along before we had her, and can't imagine what we would do without her."

Guest speakers galore delighted the 2500 adults who attended the convention at the Palmer House in Chicago.

...Reorganizes Into Divisions

La Leche League's growth and development is remarkable by any standards. From one group in Franklin Park in 1956 to more than 3,300 groups in the United States and 42 foreign countries in 1977. From seven leaders in 1956 to well over 10,000 leaders in 1977. The founding mothers are the first to admit that none of it was planned or expected. It just happened.

"It seemed that this was just something that had to go on at this time," Edwina said. "No one was more inefficient than we were because we just couldn't be efficient. We weren't equipped, we were working from our homes, it was hard to get together, and with small children our time was not our own.

"We simply were not able to do all of the things with our organization that most people would do. But we felt that we were into something that was meant to be. When needs presented themselves as the organization grew we would try to respond to them. That was the best we could do.

"We never sat down and made a plan because we never had time for that. We were all at home with our kids and there was just no time to plan this organization. It was always a question of just trying to keep up with what we were being confronted with at the moment. It was always what the biggest need was at the moment. Whatever the most phone calls and the most letters were about was the thing you had to come to grips with right away.

"It has only been in the last few years when our children didn't need as much of our time that we got down to more organization and system and planning. It is only now with three or four founding mothers working together in the office where we can easily confer with each other that it has been possible to do some planning."

The changes that have occurred as the founding mothers were able to spend more time planning are

"We felt that we were into something that was meant to be."

particularly apparent in the evolution of the League's organizational structure. In the beginning, the limited amount of time they had to give was taken by the demands of the groups in Franklin Park, so any woman who asked to start her own La Leche League group was told to go ahead on her own and run her group pretty much as she chose. It wasn't until the mid-sixties that the founding mothers were able to begin working in earnest to qualify the women who wished to represent La Leche League. It was 1964 before the position of Executive Coordinator was established to provide assistance and guidance for group leaders. It was the early 1970s before the organization had progressed to the point that every state had state-level officers.

The intensive growth of La Leche League in the 1970s necessitated yet another major organizational change. One person, the LLLI Executive Coordinator, had been carrying the responsibility for all La Leche League groups and leaders, as well as being the head of the CLA department. But as the number of League groups mushroomed in the 1970s, it was no longer feasible for one person to handle this job.

On April 1, 1976, the Executive Coordinator Department was reorganized into five separate departments—Eastern United States (East of the Mississippi River); Western United States (West of the Mississippi River); Canada; Around the World; and the CLA Department.

Mary Ann Bytnar was selected to head the Western Division.

"She had been a member of the LLLI Committee and knew a lot about area organization and League philosophy and policy," Betty said. "She had so much experience and so much to offer that she was one of the first ones we thought of to head up a Division."

Judy Good was tapped as Eastern Regional Director.

"Judy had been the area coordinator for Ohio for many years," Betty said. "Ohio has more groups than any other Area in the world. Ohio League groups have grown and spread at a fantastic rate, and we felt that if she could manage that large state so well she would be great for the entire Eastern Division. And she has been!"

Margaret Bennet-Alder had been Area Coordinator for Canada prior to the reorganization.

"She was the most knowledgeable about Canada, and we were sure she would do a great job, so we just changed her title and she became head of the Canadian Division," Betty explained.

Ruth Sanecki took charge of the Around The World Division.

"Ruth knew just about everything about League," Betty said. "She had been Illinois State Coordinator, a member of the LLLI Committee, and had some experience in nearly every aspect of LLL. We knew she had the background and experience to handle whatever might come up in the Around The World Division."

The CLA Department was put under founding mother Mary Ann Cahill's direction.

"We knew Mary Ann understood League philosophy, and we felt that because she was such a talented writer she would be able to communicate the philosophy to leader applicants. She was a natural choice for the post, and she was willing and eager to boot!"

It was recognized that dividing the League administratively into four geographical divisions would result in some procedural differences between the divisions, but it was felt that this amount of flexibility could be advantageous.

When it came to the CLA Department, however, it was thought that it was important to maintain uniformity in the principles and methods of certifying leaders, and it was therefore kept under one director.

The position of Regional Director was also established, the Regions being geographical units smaller than the divisions, but larger than individual states or provinces. Regional Directors were appointed not only in the Coordinating and CLA Departments but in the Professional Liaison Department as well. They serve as assistants to the Coordinating Director or department head concerned, and are responsible to them.

"With Regional Directors, if there is a problem in that region, they're living right there and are much more likely to recognize it than somebody in Columbus or Toronto or the Chicago area who is corresponding with someone there," Betty explained. "We believe that this reorganization is helping us to more effectively help the mothers who want to breastfeed their babies."

...Writes A Leader's Handbook

In the early years, being a League leader was pretty much a "learn as you go" experience. Leaders, especially those who lived outside of the Chicago area, were essentially on their own. The process of qualifying women for leadership evolved fairly rapidly to a point where by the time they received their certificate they were familiar with, and in agreement with, basic League philosophy, and had a general idea of how to lead a group and help individual mothers with breastfeeding. But the wealth of information and experience which accumulated as the League developed and grew was not available to all of them equally. Some were in touch with an individual experienced leader, or a strong state organization, which could share information with them; but even then, this varied from one area to another.

By the late 1960s, nearly every level and department in League had much to share with leaders to help them do their jobs—information about managing a group, helping mothers, organizing group workers, and being an effective La Leche League representative. But although the information leaders needed was usually there—somewhere—they didn't always know where to find it when they needed it.

When LEAVEN began appearing in 1965, it helped disseminate some of this material; and LEAVEN went to all leaders, so they all benefited from it. But LEAVEN couldn't cover everything in one issue, or in many issues, and the particular information a leader might need at a particular time was still often hard to come by.

It was in 1966 that Lorrie Dyal, Leslie Hawkinson, and Judy Kahrl, who later comprised the LLLI Writing and Research Committee, saw the need to compile and organize existing material, add some important information that wasn't written down at all, and put it all together for the leaders.

"Lorrie and Judy flew into Franklin Park and discussed the idea with us," Edwina recalled. "They had conducted an informal study, determined what the needs were, and suggested that a leader's handbook was what was needed. We thought it was a great idea."

The three women set to work, but the project soon began running into one obstacle after another.

"There wasn't enough money to bring them in often enough to really get it going," Edwina said. "There were many delays because several of the women working on it either at their end or ours had family responsibilities that periodically took up a great deal of their time. And for a long time we couldn't come up with enough money to publish it."

After contributing much time and work to the project, Lorrie and Leslie went on to other League duties, leaving the job of compiling and pulling it together in Judy's hands.

At long last the pieces began to fall into place. It was decided to issue the handbook in loose leaf form, a chapter or two at a time. Again Maurice Cattani of the Mary Jane Company generously furnished funds for a League project, and early in 1977 Chapters I and II of the LEADER'S HANDBOOK were published and distributed to active leaders. These two chapters contain the basic information pertaining to group organization and group meetings.

"When I think back over all the obstacles, it was a triumphant moment!" Judy said.

In June, 1977, another section of the Handbook, Chapter V, "Communicator's Guide," prepared by Public Relations Director Faye Young and Paula Kirkpatrick, was published and made available for leaders to add to their Handbooks.

Chapter III, dealing with special meetings (fathers', couples', toddlers, etc.), Chapter IV, "Mother to Mother Help," and Chapter VI, "Outreach into the Community," are still in process.

...Expands Its Reference Library

When the founding mothers organized La Leche League in 1956, their library consisted primarily of brief paragraphs from medical textbooks and articles from *Child-Family Digest* and a few other magazines, housed in a cardboard box. Today that library has grown into a flourishing reference center with information on all aspects of breastfeeding.

"We have been slowly collecting books and articles on breastfeeding and related subjects," Edwina said. "Our library has become quite extensive. People tell us that it is probably the most complete collection in this special area anywhere."

It is big and complex enough to keep reference librarian Carolyn Hayes very busy. She estimates that the LLLI office receives an average of two hundred telephone requests and three hundred written requests for references each year. And of course there is a steady stream of requests for resource material from within the organization. Publications Department in particular leans heavily on Carolyn for references when an LLLI Information Sheet on a technical subject is being written or revised.

From a cardboard box to an extensive library — the LLLI reference center, like La Leche League itself, developed and grew out of the founding mothers' commitment to do whatever they could to help any woman, anywhere, nurse her baby.

...Looks For Funding

When La Leche League consisted of two or three groups, the modest dues collected from mothers attending meetings were sufficient to meet their modest expenses. But as the number of groups grew, and grew, and grew, the organization necessary to supply them with leadership and encouragement and information had to expand more and more, and additional sources of revenue had to be found.

Today, LLLI's main source of income is from sales of manuals, cookbooks, reprints, etc. Money is also derived from NEWS and LEAVEN subscriptions, but all of this goes for their production and mailing. Donations represent a smaller but significant source. The generous gifts sent in response to the annual appeal letter meet some pressing needs; several bequests have been received also, and it seems that more and more friends of the League are beginning to mention it in their wills. But LLLI's worldwide commitments continue to grow, and the need for more money becomes more urgent.

"If we are going to get into Europe and Asia, we will need foundation money," Vi Lennon explained. "We are working hard to get foundations to contribute money to the League."

Vi's position of Special Projects Coordinator was created about a year and a half ago, primarily for the purpose of seeking out foundation money.

"I'm all for the Boy Scouts and Boys' Clubs," Vi said, "but I think we also have an important service to offer. We start at the beginning of life. I think that the people who are in League are getting tremendous amounts of information and encouragement toward really good mothering. By helping them give their babies the best start in life, we are making an enormous contribution to society."

...Works With Friends And Relatives

As the LLLI office staff grew one person had to be in charge and Betty and Edwina readily agreed between them that Betty would be that person. Betty remained as office manager, as well as LLLI Treasurer, until 1971 when her other League work increased to the point where it became impossible for her to also function as manager of the ever increasing office staff.

At that time, Mr. James Puchner, an accountant-friend of Betty and Edwina, whose office was in the same building and who had for some time been helping with LLLI accounting, offered to take over as office manager. It was an economical arrangement for LLLI, since Jim could give part of every day to LLLI work and still handle his own business. There was no way that LLLI could have paid the kind of salary Jim could have commanded for the time and expertise he gave; because he is the kind of person who believes in making a contribution to society, he charged LLLI a mere pittance.

Besides performing the general overseeing and trouble-shooting functions of an office manager, Jim made three major contributions to the efficient operation of the LLLI office: he codified and set down LLLI personnel policies; assumed the burden of planning and supervising the extensive remodeling of 9616 Minneapolis; and oversaw the purchase, installation, and training of personnel for the computer made necessary by the burgeoning work of the Order Department.

In 1975 Jim resigned to devote full time to his own business, and Bernie Heimos, Marian's aunt, who had long been the cheery voice on the reception office phone, took over as office manager.

"Family first" is a League slogan familiar to all LLLers, but they may not be aware that it extends to the employment practices in the LLLI office. In many organizations there are stern rules against the employment of more than one member of the same family; but at LLLI, nepotism reigns supreme. The *Personnel Policies* booklet specifically lists the order for hiring, qualifications being equal:

1. Founding Mother's child
2. Other Board Member's child
3. LLL Mothers (other than Board members)
4. Children of LLL Mothers and Employees
5. Relatives of above (in same order)
6. Friends or neighbors of above (in same order)

This policy has worked out well. Whether it be relative or friend, if the person is capable and has the time to devote to the job, it saves LLLI advertising, paying an agency, and checking on references.

For example, in 1965 when we needed someone to take charge of NEWS circulation, Marian mentioned that her widowed mother was a hard worker and was not very happy at the place she was working. Marie Leonard came in and took over and has been working hard for LLLI ever since. Later, when we needed someone in the front office at the reception desk, and to handle the many incoming calls, Marie said her sister might like the job. Bernie had held a number of jobs in the past but at that particular time was not employed. Now, Bernie as office manager in charge of personnel, still employs the tactic of asking around when a new employee is needed. Occasionally we have to advertise, but more often it is someone's neighbor or relative who gets the job. In addition to all matters regarding the personnel of the office, Bernie also handles the payroll and a portion of the bookkeeping. In 1966, when someone especially good at organization and detail work was needed to take care of shipping, Marie recommended her friend Doris Ditchkus, and Doris has kept on top of an exacting — and always growing — job ever since.

You may be interested in knowing all who are working at LLLI at this point, and how they are interrelated. Here they are, by departments:

ADMINISTRATION
Marian Tompson, President; Betty Wagner, Administrator-Treasurer; Edwina Froehlich, Executive Secretary; Bernie Heimos, Office Manager.
Part-time: Viola Lennon, Chairman of the Board and Special Projects Director; Mary Ann Cahill, Director of CLA Department.

CIRCULATION
Marie Leonard, Supervisor (Marian Tompson's mother), Laurel Davies (Marian's daugher), Dorothy Gale (who answered an ad), Pat Grabanski (friend of Doris Ditchkus), Millie Mlynarski (neighbor of Harriet Modrich), Irene Yarosh (friend of Marie). They keep the files of NEWS and LEAVEN subscribers, ACs, CLAs, PAB members, APLs, HRT trainers, and other special lists; address, sort, zip, and tie each mailing and get it ready for the post office.

INFORMATION
Bernie Heimos, Supervisor (Marian Tompson's aunt), handles special appeals and donations, Joyce Kasheimer (sister of Jean Henkel) and Bonnie Alt (answered an ad) handle the reception room and incoming phone calls. They keep the files of leaders and groups up to date and keep track of and distribute CLA supplies. Cecilia Moore (friend of Marie Leonard) is a typist and general clerical worker in this department.

LLL leaders Harriet Modrich, who was part of the original League group that met at Mary White's house, and Annamae Boutin answer mothers' phone calls for breastfeeding help and information. Harriet also catalogs the books and magazines for the nonmedical section of our library. Annamae coordinates the letterwriters for LLLI, handles requests for LLLI exhibits, materials for the blind, and the LLLI Information Service materials.

ORDER
Eileen Appler, Supervisor (Betty Wagner's cousin), Marge Berg (answered an ad), Jean Henkel (relative of a neighbor of Marybeth Doucette), Diana Grinvalds (neighbor of Edwina), Fran Libel (friend of Eileen), and The Computer (friend of Jim Puchner), receive, record, and dispatch order forms to Shipping, and handle billing and accounts receivable. Jean also assists in accounting and payroll.

PUBLICATIONS
Mary Carson, Supervisor, Marybeth Doucette, LaVerne Spadaro (LLL's first employee — remember?), and Judy Torgus edit, typeset, and lay out NEWS, LEAVEN, and all other LLLI publications, including Information Sheets, lists, flyers, forms — if it's printed and LLLI sends it out, it passes through the hands of the Publications Department. NEWS circulation has now reached 50,000 and LEAVEN 11,000.

Working closely with Publications is Barbara Horan, who is in charge of translations of our materials. The growing demand for LLL publications in different languages began a number of years ago, and Judy Bernetzke handled their preparation until 1972, when Barbara took over. A number of LLLI publications are now available in Danish, French, German, Hebrew, Italian, Japanese, Portuguese, Spanish, and Vietnamese.

Another special aspect of Publications is the provision of materials for the blind in braille and/or on tape. Different mothers have been working on this since the mid-sixties — Johanna Horton, Dianne Adams, Kathy Beaudette, Diane Dollak, Mary Hiland come to mind. In 1972 this work was given a tremendous impetus when a non-League friend, Marilyn Lap, who devotes much of her time to providing blind persons with brailled or taped materials they need which are not available to them elsewhere, perceived the usefulness of League materials for blind mothers and in connection with her own service took over the brailling, taping, and distribution of practically all League materials. More recently the distribution of these has been channeled through the LLLI office, where Annamae Boutin is in charge of them. Marilyn continues to do the taping of NEWS and LEAVEN for us.

REFERENCE/RESEARCH
Marian Tompson, Supervisor. Carolyn Hayes (friend of Mary Carson's daughter) is in charge of LLLI's reference library of breastfeeding information and related subjects; processes and keeps files on requests for cooperating with medical research; handles the detail work for the Physicians' Seminars and the Paul György Award; helps Publications and Stenographic Departments with translations of French and Spanish correspondence and articles and with proofreading.

SHIPPING (and MIMEOGRAPHING)
Doris Ditchkus, Supervisor (friend of Marie Leonard). Evelynne Lostumo (neighbor of Edwina), Vicki Panek (friend of Pat Grabanski), Carol Schafer (friend of Joyce Kasheimer), Edna Schuelke (answered an ad), Alice Severyns (sister of Millie Mlynarski), Joan Simonetta (answered an ad), Pauline Sirotzke (friend of Joyce), receive the orders from Order Department and ship out the books, reprints, and other materials handled by LLLI. Doris is also in charge of mimeographing, assisted by Edna. She does the ordering for the office as well.

STENOGRAPHIC
Edwina Froehlich, Supervisor. Shirley Biancalana (neighbor of Edwina), Fran Cassano (neighbor of Diane Holzer), and Diane Holzer (answered an ad), are responsible for typing final copies of all mailings from the Administrator, the Board of Directors, Coordinating Directors, and Department Heads, do secretarial work and filing for the executives, and are responsible for various other record-keeping and scheduling activities.

MAINTENANCE
Gina Krenz (neighbor of an LLL leader) keeps the lunchroom and conference room sparkling during the week and fills in as a helper sorting, mimeographing, and various odd jobs as needed. David Froehlich (Edwina's son), disposes of rubbish and cleans the offices on weekends.

PART-TIME HELP
Especially during the summer vacation period, a number of other helpers work at LLLI: Ralph Berg (Marge's son), Rosemarie Doucette (Marybeth's daughter), Peter Froehlich (Edwina's son), Sharon Henkel (Jean's daughter), Joe Sirotzke (Pauline's husband), Brian Tompson (Marian's son), Dorothy and Helen Wagner (Betty's daughters), Beth Hasse (Helen's friend), Mary Cecilia and Michael White (Mary's daughter and son) are among the "regulars."

CONSULTANTS
Chuck Cahill (Mary Ann's husband) has helped out with accounting from the beginning.

Dr. Herbert Ratner, Senior Medical Consultant to the League, comes to the office one day a week. Ed Roberts (business associate of Jim Puchner), serves as a consultant on printing, publishing, and budget.

Edmund M. Tobin (Marian's cousin) assists with general legal advice. Milton A. Levenfeld (friend of Chuck Cahill), serves as a consultant on tax matters.

Other "consultants" who should be mentioned, though they are not on the LLLI payroll, are our printers, who through the years have given us much constructive advice and help. John Hudetz of Solar Press (LA LECHE LEAGUE NEWS, LEADER'S HANDBOOK, and many special Information Sheets and other materials); Hans Paulsen of Interstate Printers & Publishers (THE WOMANLY ART OF BREASTFEEDING and MOTHER'S IN THE KITCHEN); Joe Schrippe of Westward-Ho Press (LEAVEN and many Information Sheets and special jobs); Hank Mashke of Johnson Printers (LLLI Fact Folder, Conference materials — registration forms, programs, souvenir albums, etc. — and this book, THE LLLOVE STORY). Hank is now sporting several new grey hairs, but insists he llloved helping us put out THE LLLOVE STORY.

We are proud of our office and all the friendly people who work here. We want the LLLI Office to be a happy, pleasant place to work in and we treat our employees as friends and neighbors (which they often are before they become employees). Most of us in the Office are also mothers and we have set our office hours to accommodate this fact. Most work from 7 to 3, or 9 to 3. There is never a problem of taking time off to tend to a sick child or other family needs. Our employees don't have to call in sick when they need a day off for other reasons. But no one abuses this trust we place in them and work is done with care and speed.

Of course in the handling of 100,000 pieces of mail (incoming) last year plus the recording and shipping of thousands of orders, mountains of mimeographing, and answering hundreds of letters, we do have some mixups as mistakes are bound to happen. But LLLI Office people take a pride in their work, they feel badly when mistakes are made and try very hard to avoid them.

Our employees like the personal touch in their jobs — the notes that come with the orders sometimes, and when now and then someone writes us a letter of praise, it gets passed around and ends up on the bulletin board and makes everyone feel good for the rest of the week.

Because we are a small office we can have some fun that might not be possible in a larger office with twice as many people. For example, we celebrate birthdays. All those who have birthdays occurring in the month get together and decide which day that month they will treat the office. When the day arrives the loud speaker calls everyone to the kitchen to wish Whoever a Happy Birthday. The birthday women lay their spread out and act as hostesses (as well as cleanup crew) and we all wish them well as we munch their delicious goodies.

The downstairs personnel treats the upstairs to a Valentine Day luncheon every year — a gorgeous pot luck spread. For Halloween the upstairs treats the downstairs. Last year at 11:45 A.M. everyone donned costumes for the Halloween luncheon and

Where else but the LLLI Office could you find everyone from Mother Superior (Edwina, far left) to a wide-eyed peasant lady (Bernie Heimos, lower left).

Halloween potluck spread. Marie Leonard is in right foreground.

some of the homemade outfits made for a really hilarious celebration.

During the month of December each department takes a different day to host a Christmas snack party, and every department puts up their own decorations — some are very glamorous and sparkly, some extremely creative, and then some of us put up some kind of tacky stuff—but it is all in good spirit. The parties on these special days take a bit of extra time, as compared to the usual half-hour, but everyone tries to work extra hard to make up, and these parties do tend to help our office morale. Moreover, each employee is quite aware of certain jobs that MUST be done on that day, party or no party. And these special times provide a refreshing break in the routine and lead to better understanding, cooperation, and friendships between the departments (to say nothing of lots of recipe swapping).

If you happen to be in the neighborhood of our office some time between the hours of 7 and 3 Monday through Friday, drop in and we will enjoy showing you around. We are sure you will find it interesting and we would love to have you.

Betty and Edwina

Christmas festivities at the LLLI Office — Bonnie Alt, Annamae Boutin, Peggy Wagner, Cecilia Moore, and Joyce Kasheimer.

In The Years To Come...

What does La Leche League plan to do in the years ahead? Continue as we always have — meeting the needs of breastfeeding mothers and their babies. This will still be done primarily through monthly meetings held in homes. While in the past most of these meetings have been for women only, a growing number are being offered for both husband and wife.

Nursing mothers will continue to be able to get answers to their questions by telephone on a round-the-clock basis, and we will continue to provide additional information through our numerous publications and through our breastfeeding seminars.

In recent years we have found ourselves becoming more and more involved on a public level in refuting the arguments that are sometimes used to attack breast milk as the most suitable food for infants. Keeping informed about these issues and educating the public about them seems to have become our responsibility as the spokesperson for breastfeeding mothers.

We are also finding that La Leche League is being used with increasing frequency as a breastfeeding resource at the local, national, and international levels by hospitals, universities, and government agencies.

It is gratifying to watch breastfeeding become more common in a number of countries, and to know that we have played some part in this trend. But there is still much to be done, and we know that the expertise of the League will be in demand for many years to come.

The world will always need the special kind of love and sharing that characterizes the La Leche League leader. I can't help but rejoice in this continuing opportunity we have as wives and mothers to change the world.

Marian Tompson

The Seven Speak for Themselves

They have changed our lives, these seven women who founded La Leche League. We came wanting to learn the art of breastfeeding. We found a way of life.

We marvel at all they have accomplished. We strive to live up to the ideals they have presented. We are deeply grateful for the richness they have brought into our lives. How often we have wished we could know personally these women who have had such an impact on our lives.

You have met each of the founders in this book, and gained new insights into who each one is and what she has contributed to LLL. But before we close, we have asked each founding mother to tell you, in her own words, about herself, her family, and her life.

The Cahills

In 1956 when the phone calls began going back and forth in Franklin Park on "getting together to talk about nursing babies" (the word "breastfeeding" was avoided), a working day would start for the Cahills with Chuck going to his job as the accountant for a construction firm in a nearby suburb. Baby Mary, born in December of 1955, would be nursed, changed, and placed in her favorite spot in the kitchen by the cuckoo clock and near the door where she was greeted by the older kids as they came down for breakfast.

Bob and Elizabeth were in the primary grades and walked to the local school. Tim, age four, and Teresa, three, were "still home with Mama." Tim and Teresa are the closest in age, sixteen months apart, which had worried me when I became pregnant with Teresa. As it turned out, they were the most compatible — Teresa's outgoingness making up for Tim's shyness.

There was plenty for me to do at home. Getting a load of wash going first thing after breakfast was an everyday routine. No one dreamed of mothers having an outside job. It wasn't done in those days. Mothers stayed home and "kept house," especially with babies coming every few years.

Large families were a switch from the general pattern of the depression years when I grew up, one of two children. The announcement of yet another baby due, once past number three, would often draw a response akin to, "I'm glad it's you and not me."

Yet we were far from alone in raising our brood. A good number of other young couples in the community were going through the same joys and frustrations, and Chuck and I and other parents in the "Station Wagon Set" found each other through CFM (Christian Family Movement). A sense of camaraderie developed as we coped with feeding the hungry and clothing the naked — mostly our own offspring.

In general I remember the feeling of the time as being "Things are good and getting better." Young couples were meeting together in CFM and looking for ways to promote happier family life. The Whites had invited us to our first CFM meeting. If only in a small way, the ordinary person felt he could change the world. When the seven of us mothers started the nursing mothers group named La Leche League, we were not thinking of founding a world-wide organization, but then again I don't think we ever doubted that we could manage the challenges of the day.

There was no excess of material things, but then we certainly never went without necessities. Families started with furniture dubbed "Early Salvation Army," or as in our case, "Recycled From The Relatives." When we were expecting our firstborn, Elizabeth, Chuck was still in school and only worked part time. She was born at a Catholic maternity hospital that charged according to one's means. Cost of doctor and hospital — $60.00.

Also, our families were a great help. Grandparents, brothers and sisters lived nearby and we saw them often. When the laundry piled up to what looked like sixteen tons, Grandma always seemed to appear on the scene and with quick efficiency set things to order.

Today the Cahills live in Libertyville, the town we chose as we searched for bigger housing for our family. We were nine when we moved in 1960. Margaret was the baby and our Good Will Ambassador with a six month old's propensity to smile for everyone. Three year old Joe, our first home delivery, had arrived the October Dr. Grantly Dick-Read spoke in Franklin Park. Chuck was starting his own accounting business.

Our two youngest were born here at home in Libertyville, thanks to the accommodating Dr. White. Charlie (Charlene) arrived on a lovely August afternoon in 1963 with the neighborhood kids waiting on the front porch for the announcement. Frances, the youngest, was born two years later, again with my mainstay, Chuck, at my side, and Dr. White, keeping a careful watch over the birth process, nearby. As the family grew, it was heartwarming to see the older ones respond to a baby with tenderness and tolerance. Once out of the baby stage, we had our share of kids bickering, but those children grew up and are the best of friends. They go off into the world and bring the world back to us.

The grandparents are gone, and now we are announcing weddings instead of baptisms. Three are now married, and we have three grandchildren. When Teresa had her firstborn, breastfeeding was as natural to her as breathing. There have been many celebrations, some tears. But it's always a grand time when we're all together — and thank goodness for the dishwasher!

A local nursing mother had received my name from Franklin Park and was the second to knock on our door, a milkman being the first, after we had moved in. Paula Pettengill and I started a League group in Libertyville; eventually groups were started in five neighboring towns. By then my League hours were mainly devoted to group work, since I found it difficult to travel the 27 miles to Franklin Park for the then almost weekly Board Meetings.

My first love will always be the group, meeting with other mothers, sharing the wonders of babies and breastfeeding. It's like the early days of the League, with the seven of us meeting and planning together in the Whites' living room. You KNOW being a mother is important.

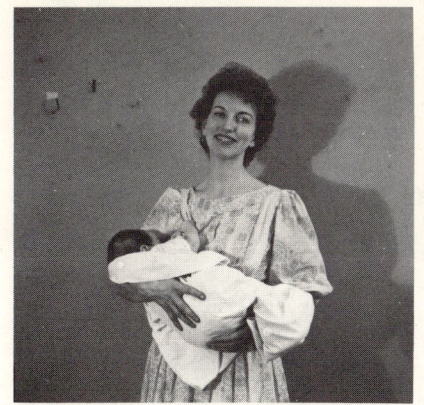

Mary Ann and baby Margaret, 1960.

Princess Grace, Mary Ann and Betty at the 1971 convention.

Bobby and Elizabeth with Chuck; Mary Ann holding Tim.

Margaret looks on as Mary Ann nurses Charlie.

The Cahills in 1962 — Chuck, Margaret, Joe, Mary, Teresa, Tim, Bob, Elizabeth and Mary Ann.

Mary Ann in front of the Wagners' home with Helen Wagner, Charlie and Fran.

The Cahills in 1973 at Elizabeth's wedding.

77

The Froehlichs

Paul was an active six-year-old and we were the proud parents of our first kindergartner in 1956. David was three and still keeping mom company at home. Home was 3332 Rose Street, situated just a half block from the big public high school. Many community clubs held their meetings there. I joined the Women's Club at first. It was easy to attend an evening program because it was so close to home, and once the boys were bedded down John was happy to babysit while resting comfortably in his easy chair. Later I joined the Women's Civic Club, which was doing some things for the community which I thought were important. It was there I met Mary Carson, who has been our Publications Director for some years. I remember that the first time she talked at a Club meeting I was so impressed with her knowledge and creativity. Little did I know how closely we would one day work together and how very much I would learn from her.

In Chicago we had belonged to a Christian Family organization in connection with our church. We used to meet once a month in each others' homes. In the apartment building we lived in we exchanged sitter services. It was an ideal arrangement because we were all mothers, and our children played with each other during the day. We traded hours only — no money — and kept strict accounting. When Mary White phoned to invite us to join a similar group in Franklin Park, she told me that they too had an exchange sitter service involving the mothers. So I promptly signed up, and the first young mother who came to sit for us on meeting night was Marian Tompson, who at that time had three children. Subsequently I met Mary Ann Cahill, Betty Wagner and Mary Ann Kerwin. (I had known Vi Lennon previously.)

Even though I was not breastfeeding when I met these women, breastfeeding was a common bond that gave us almost instant rapport.

On the Monday after the famous weekend picnic (I can't remember why I wasn't there—maybe we had chickenpox or something) Marian called me and told about the many mothers at the picnic who had approached her and Mary as they nursed, to express their disappointment at not being able to do the same. Marian reported that they decided the time had come to do something about it and that they had set a date for a get-together at Mary's house the following week. As one author wrote of us—"In true American fashion, they organized!"

Everyone at that meeting was either pregnant or nursing a baby. John and I were very eager to have another child before our time ran out (I was thirty-four when Paul was born), and I can recall mentioning to him that if I didn't get pregnant pretty soon I just didn't know whether I could stay with the group—my yearning for a baby was too great. It wasn't long after that when we conceived Peter, our last child. When Peter was born I really belonged to that group of women in a special way.

Peter was born at home, as were the other two boys. Drs. Ratner and White were on hand when Paul and David were born in our third floor walk-up in Chicago. Peter arrived at our Franklin Park house at 3332 Rose Street, which a year later became the first official address of La Leche League. As the secretary I answered the letters and received the mail. My office was my desk and typewriter in the corner of our dining room. For about ten years that dining room was an organized mess of stationery, carbon paper, stamps, books, diapers, safety pins, and snacks.

Twenty years later we live in a newer house several blocks south. Since it has no dining room it is fortunate that La Leche meanwhile acquired an office just a couple of blocks from home.

Paul is twenty-six—teaches history and political science and coaches wrestling at an all-boy high school in Chicago. David is twenty-three and teaches physical education and health and coaches wrestling at a public high school in a nearby suburb. Peter is nineteen and studying (and wrestling) at the University of Illinois. Their wrestling, which started out in that big living room in the old house on Rose street, paid off in college scholarships, and David managed to make All American one year. Paul will be married in June to Marilyn, a lovely young woman who went to the same high school and lives nearby. His marriage will be as exciting to us as his first day at kindergarten—another milestone for him and for his parents. The oldest child is ever the pioneer in the family—he undertakes all the firsts and makes it easier for the siblings who follow.

I still leave the house in the morning after everyone else, just as I did when I first started to work at the office when Peter went to first grade. The only difference is that for some years now I have not had a son to meet on the corner at noon and again at 3 o'clock as I did all the years they were in grammar school.

Even though our family was a relatively small one, there was always a stream of children going in and out. It is now a pleasure to welcome the grown-up children who are friends of our sons. Gone is the roughhouse that often tried our patience and was hard on the furniture, but we still enjoy the conversation and the laughter, and hope we'll always have it to some extent at least. All in all, it has been a good twenty years for the Froehlich family. 'Twasn't always easy — but we wouldn't trade it for anything.

The Froehlichs in 1956 — John, Edwina, Paul and David.

Paul at twenty-one months, 1952.

The Froehlichs in 1962 in their dining room that did double duty as League's office — David, John, Peter, Edwina, Paul.

Peter snoozing in Edwina's lap, 1957.

Paul with fiancee Marilyn, 1977.

The Froehlichs in 1977 — Edwina and Paul's fiancee, Marilyn; David, Peter, John and Paul.

79

The Kerwins

I was married to my husband, Tom, a young lawyer at Christmastime in 1954. After graduating with a B.A. in literature from Barat College in Lake Forest, Illinois, I did some teaching and then worked as a travel agent. I was ready to settle down and raise a family, and fortunately the right man came along.

After we were married, I couldn't wait to get pregnant. It seemed a long eleven months waiting for our first child, a son, who was born on his maternal grandmother's birthday. In 1955 husbands were never allowed in the delivery room and I knew I'd do a much better job of giving birth if Tom was with me. So Tom and I planned for a home delivery in our third floor walk-up apartment.

We were invited out to dinner and a dance while I was in the beginning stages of labor. I assumed it would be a long first stage so we went anyway and had a lovely time, with Tom discreetly helping me with occasional strong contractions.

Wisely, we decided to skip the dance and go home. Almost immediately things started happening indicating our baby might really be on his way. Dr. White arrived in seemingly no time at all, and we all concentrated on giving birth. Tom and I were ecstatic at the birth of our first son, Thomas More! We just couldn't believe that this experience of which we had heard so many horror stories would be so totally joyous.

I had a difficult start with breastfeeding, probably because I didn't even know how to hold a baby. With a great deal of patient help from Greg and Mary White, I finally got started, despite having reached such an engorged stage that it was difficult for my baby to grasp the nipple. During those first days it was so ironic that I was dripping with milk and none was getting into my baby's mouth. With the Whites' help, as well as encouragement from my husband and mother, we finally got going.

> **"I had a difficult start with breastfeeding, probably because I didn't even know how to hold a baby."**

I had been happily nursing our son and was pregnant with our second baby when Mary White asked me if I would like to help start a group for breastfeeding mothers.

Mary and Greg White had given me so much support and encouragement as well as practical advice about breastfeeding. I never would have succeeded without them. With this kind of background I felt eager to help other mothers less fortunate than myself, and also I enjoyed the thought of discussions with other breastfeeding mothers from whom I could learn and exchange information and ideas. I immediately thought that was a wonderful idea and enthusiastically said "yes."

Our second son, Edward, was born in 1957. Our third son, Joseph, was born in 1959. He was a big, healthy baby, but at the age of five weeks I found our apparently thriving little baby dead in his bassinet after having nursed him to sleep several hours earlier. He was a victim of the now-designated "Sudden Infant Death Syndrome."

We were heartbroken over the death of this very much wanted little boy. But as I wrote to our League friends who were so very kind, generous and thoughtful, "Through League, we are learning and teaching true motherhood. We have been asked to understand one more aspect of it... The Earth and its fullness are the Lord's."

After Joe's death, my arms felt so empty and my breasts so full. Even this extreme shock didn't cause me to lose my abundant supply of milk.

Our other six children were born in Denver with Dr. Robert Bradley attending. I always missed my own bed and familiar surroundings, but I was allowed to leave the hospital two hours after delivery.

Today there seems to be an extraordinary feeling of family unity among our children, with the older children helping, encouraging and enjoying the younger ones. Even as the older boys have gone off to college, we remain a close-knit family.

Tom, twenty-one, graduated this year from Colorado College with a political science major. Ed, nineteen, is a sophomore at Colorado College and is headed toward a science or math major. Greg, seventeen, graduated this spring from St. Regis High School as Outstanding Senior. Mary, fifteen, is a sophomore at St. Mary's High School. Anne, thirteen, just graduated from eighth grade. Katie is eleven and a sixth grader. John is in third grade, and Mike is six and in first grade. He tries very hard to keep up with everyone else, at the same time enjoying his special privilege of being the youngest. Each baby nursed longer and, of course, Mike won the race!

We're most grateful for our family. They enjoy each other, and we enjoy them, each in a unique way. Despite the day-to-day struggles of trying to keep up with their myriad activities, finding time for each child, keeping nutritious food on the table, clean laundry in circulation, we wouldn't trade our situation for any other.

Mary Ann, Tom and Tommy, summer of 1956.

John, Anne, Mary Ann, Mary, Katie, and Michael at Aspen, 1975.

Tom, Mary Ann, Anne, Tom Sr., Mary, Ed, Greg, 1964.

The gang's all here — Tom, John, Ed, Michael, Mary Ann, Greg, Tom Sr., Anne, Mary, Katie.

Vi with Gina, Edwina, Mary Ann Cahill, Betty Wagner, Mary Ann Kerwin with Katie, in front of the Kerwins' home in Denver, Colorado.

The Kerwins in 1976 — Mary Ann, Michael, Ed, Greg, Mary, Tom Sr., Katie, Anne, John, and Tom.

81

The Lennons

On looking back into these years, I now realize how valuable this period was for nurturing my newly found ideas on mothering and giving the children an easy and comfortable belief that "Breastfed is best fed." In the early years, I felt uncomfortable nursing a baby outside of my home. I remember thinking it would be a good idea to have venetian blinds on the car. For the children, raised with a mother often nursing a baby and often finding our home populated with nursing babies and their mothers, this idea of breastfeeding was naturally the normal thing to do.

The year of 1958 was also the year of my first home delivery. Having had three babies in the hospital and finally realizing that I did not need the cold and sterile atmosphere of an institution, but rather the peace, warmth, and security of my home, I decided that Rebecca would be born at the Lennons'. Her birth convinced me that home was the place for birth. As the years passed, more home deliveries only added to my conviction.

Rebecca's birth also added to the mystery of her 11 month older sister, Melissa. Mimi, as she insisted on being called, stopped breastfeeding at three months. She simply refused the breast. I was astonished and so were my friends. The doctor couldn't believe his eyes. We tried to starve her out, thinking she might be on a nursing strike. All our plans ended in failure and feeling rejected by my own baby, I finally and sadly made my first formula. Nine months later, Rebecca was born and to this day I am not sure what happened. So many girls have been able to nurse through a pregnancy, but it was my baby who refused me. Happily, the relationship between Mimi and her mother has improved with each passing year.

Another interesting happening at the Lennons' was the birth of the "real" twins after my experience with "Irish" twins. During this pregnancy I had not felt well, a complaint I never had through five pregnancies. Finally ending up in the hospital and fifty tests later, I was sent for an X-ray. Not even then, did it occur to me that I might be having twins. There were no twins in either family history and quite frankly, I was always delighted to have babies one at a time. When the doctor tried to explain that the picture showed "two in there," I simply refused to believe it. It seemed impossible, and the idea of taking care of two babies truly gave me feelings of panic. However, these feelings turned to real joy at their birth. Two girls, one long and dark and the other blonde and light. Interestingly, they were born on Matt's birthday. He has always felt that they were born to serve and please him, an opinion that they do not share.

Now, all is quite different in our home. We have a whole house of teenagers and young adults, with only our two youngest girls in grammar school. Martin is a sophomore in high school, with the twins going into their senior year. Matt is off to college in the Fall and those Irish twins are junior and senior college students. Mark is now a married man of four months, and Elizabeth has been married for three years. Times have so changed that my schedule now allows me two days work at the International office. It still strikes me funny that we all leave together two days a week, and quite often it is Gina, age ten, who is making Mother's lunch while I try to tidy up the kitchen.

From time to time, each of the children has helped with my League work. Of late, I have taken several of them to League affairs and each of them has shared my work in the way they like. Our newest addition to the family, Shellea, Mark's wife, now has her skills at work taking pictures at Area meetings. LLLI has been and I hope always will be a family affair.

Vi with the first of the "Irish twins," Melissa, 1956.

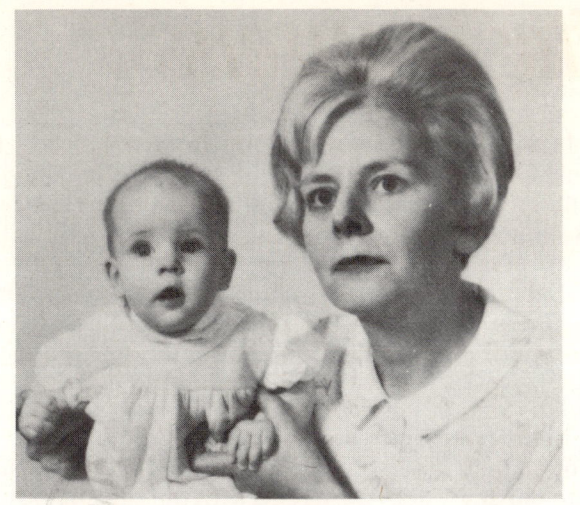

Vi with the youngest Lennon, Gina, 1967.

Vacation fun, 1967.

Santa's selections delight the little Lennons, 1962.

"Irish twins" Melissa and Rebecca.

The Lennon clan, 1974.

The Lennon's firstborn, Elizabeth, became the bride of John Zizzo, 1974.

The Tompsons

In 1956 our family lived just where we do now, in an unincorporated area of Leyden Township just outside of Franklin Park, about five minutes away from the International office. But in those days I had no car to flit around in, so I spent most of my time with our four daughters Melanie, Deborah, Allison, and Laurel (ages six and under) close to home. But I really didn't mind. I genuinely enjoyed being a wife and mother. I never was the world's greatest housekeeper, but I enjoyed cooking and baking and doing things with the girls. I particularly liked reading to them at night, and often they picked the story by the silly voice I used to portray some character. Some favorites were the LITTLE HOUSE BOOKS, C. S. Lewis' Narnia series, and Winnie the Pooh. When Daddy was home and we went out together in the car we loved to sing along the way, and through the years developed some pretty good harmony. Most of our summers were spent camping in Muskegon, Michigan — a great chance to get away and just enjoy each other.

When League started I was expecting what was to be Sheila — our fifth consecutive daughter. We also had the first of a number of foster children living with us. It wasn't always easy caring for so many. The first three girls were born in two and a half years, and I remember writing in a diary once at the end of the day about how tired I was but how much I loved those children. I had never been in an airplane except for a short piper cub flight, and my one long trip away from home was on the honeymoon Tom and I spent in Rocky Mountain National Park in Colorado.

Well, what changes the past twenty years have brought. I have traveled, not only by car, but by train, bus and airplane to most of our fifty states, and to many other countries. And all along the way the family has been very much involved in my League activities, from putting together the first edition of the manual at home to what for a long while was a weekend family activity addressing, zipping and mailing out the newsletter with everyone from father to grandmother involved. Most of the children have also worked in the League office at one time or another. Melanie, our oldest, was in the publications department until marriage took her to another city.

Three of our daughters are married now, with a fourth (away at college) to be married this summer. Tom and I have one grandchild and another on the way. Sheila lives at home, but isn't often in it, so often I'm the only female at home with Tom, Brian and Philip. Through them I'm learning about soccer, stage lighting and design, CBs, what's really wrong with the car, and other new worlds. It's a far cry from earlier days when I was also surrounded by our five daughters.

Those children we gave so much to for so long have grown up to be the kind of warm, loving people we would like to have around us even if they weren't family. And they, along with our sons-in-law and granddaughter Michelle, are the most important part of our lives.

I feel I've been very lucky in many ways. First to have the enthusiastic support of a husband who could always be called on (and frequently was) to handle jobs beyond the capabilities of seven women. And through the League to have met, and now call my friends, some of the nicest people in the world. I never expected to be president for so long and remember nostalgically my plan to introduce the new president of LLL at our first convention in 1964. Ah, WELL! It's been a busy job and seems to get more hectic by the day but also a job of much satisfaction and incredible surprises. I still find myself standing back bemused as I watch Marian Tompson deplaning in some exotic place, or chatting with Susan Saint James and Rock Hudson at Universal Studios, or answering the phone at home to find Princess Grace on the other end of the line. It's certainly a life I never expected to live, but it's a very rewarding one and also one where the flexibility Tom and I had to have as the parents of a large family continues to stand us in good stead.

The Tompson children, 1959.

The Maharajah and his slave — Philip and Laurel.

The Tompson family, 1964.

Marian and Brian, 1959.

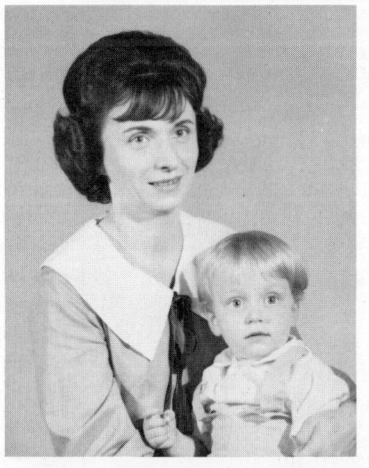

Marian and Philip, 1964.

Debbie, Laurel, Allison, and Melanie enjoy cooling off, 1956.

Daddy Tompson enjoys story time with two of his daughters.

The Tompson family at Laurel's wedding in 1974.

The Wagners

In 1956 I had four children, Gail, Robert, Wayne, Mary, and was expecting my fifth. All four of these children has been breastfed for nine or ten months. As the average suburban mother, I belonged to various women's organizations and was also involved in the PTA, and Scouts—girl, boy, and cub. We had moved to Franklin Park in 1946 when it boasted 3,000 inhabitants. During the ten years between '46 and '56 I became acquainted and then friends with Mary Ann Cahill, Edwina Froehlich, Mary White, and Marian Tompson. It was our united feelings about breastfeeding, baby and child care, and family life that brought us together to share in the beginnings of La Leche League.

When Mary Ann Cahill called to ask if I would like to join a group to help mothers who wanted to breastfeed their babies, I laughed just thinking how odd to have a breastfeeding mothers' group. I had been lucky and had always been patted on the head verbally by my attending physician for performing this natural function. I was the only one, or maybe one of two mothers, among his patients who were breastfeeding babies. All of my friends had their babies on formula and a schedule so I was always odd. How natural to join an odd group.

I hadn't had any serious problems breastfeeding. Undoubtedly, this is why I was able to continue. My mother had the right facts—she had breastfed her babies as her mother had before her. She gave all the support, advice, and encouragement that I needed. Once you have experienced the joys of breastfeeding, you do want to share this wonder with others. So I felt the group—while odd—was a wonderful idea that I immediately took to my heart. This cause soon supplanted all others and took its rightful place in importance in my life—right after my family.

During the twenty years between '56 and '76 Margaret, Dorothea, and Helen joined our family. They were all breastfed for a considerably longer period than were my first four.

These last twenty years have seen many changes in my life. My husband, Bob, died in 1975, and my five older children have married. Gail and Jack live in a nearby suburb with their six children, Bill, Matt, Pat, Jane, and the new twins Ann and Marie. Robert and Pam have moved to Florida, where they have set up a small business. Wayne, married in 1976 to Colleen, is a chef in a large office building in Chicago. Mary and Richard live nearby with daughter Kelly. Margaret, newly married to Richard (a small problem with two sons-in-law with the same first name), also lives nearby Dorothea is a recent high-school graduate headed for college, and Helen, going into her third year of high school, completes our family. I'm working full time at the LLLI office.

Our home is surely neater now than it was during the years we had the toddler shuffle. Toys have been replaced by adult games that fit neatly on a shelf. But I still have a wicker basket in the corner of the living room that contains a collection of toys to amuse my grandchildren. I like the fact that this basket will be in use for years to come. Hopefully, as long as I live.

THE BIRTH OF THE TWINS

While this book was being readied a very interesting and exciting thing happened in our family. My daughter Gail's expected baby was two days overdue. I was at the office when the call finally came for me to come to her home and take care of her older children. I grabbed my lunch and drove out as quickly as possible—about twenty-five minutes. The house was quiet when I arrived, and I found the children looking worried, sitting in their bedroom. Kelly, my daughter Mary's nine-month-old, was with them also. I asked where everyone was and the children told me in hushed tones that the baby was coming, and that Daddy, the doctor, and Mary were in with mother. With that, Mary poked her head in the door and said, "It's a girl." With three boys and one little girl already in the family, I knew Gail would be pleased to have another girl. The children and I talked about this a bit, and then they wanted to show me the hutch Bill had built for their Easter rabbit. While I was admiring it, Mary appeared breathless at the door and shouted, "There's another baby coming!" Gail had been large during this pregnancy, but she had been with past pregnancies also. Her last baby, Jane, had weighed nearly nine pounds. Gail had been assured by the doctor that she was having one very large baby. In a few minutes Mary announced another girl. You can't imagine how excited we all were. We had never had twins in our family and never expected to have them. But the doctor said they appear at about every eightieth birth. Soon their father appeared with twin number one and Mary came with twin number two. They are fraternal twins. Each weighed 7½ lbs. They looked quite a bit alike, and I was worried about mixing them up. But their father said, "What's the difference? They are both ours, so why worry?" I don't know exactly why I was worried, but I felt they shouldn't be mixed up. We finally painted Ann's toenails just to be sure she wasn't Marie. It's very satisfying to see your grandchildren receiving optimal care and nutrition at their mother's breast (as all mine have). They are both doing well now, and Gail is learning all about nursing twins.

Betty with Wayne, 1952.

Betty's oldest, Gail Gratzianna, presented the family with surprise twins, Ann and Marie, on April 14, 1977.

Helen, Dorothea, Peg, and Mary, 1962.

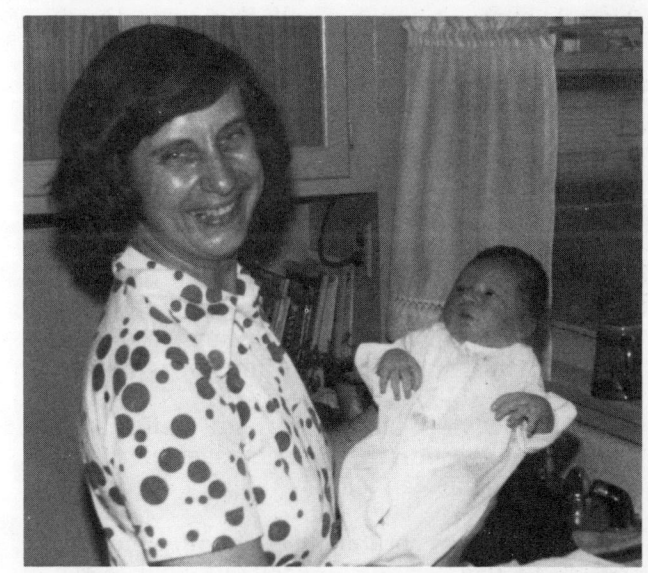

Betty with brand new granddaughter, Kelly, 1976.

Helen, age sixteen, the baby Betty is nursing in our cover photo.

The Wagners in 1971 at the wedding of their oldest son, Robert. Gail, husband Jack, and their three sons are on the right.

The Whites

When our first baby was born in 1945, in the Dark Ages, obstetrically speaking, the usual procedure was anesthesia for the delivery, with the shots, pills or what have you preceding it. We didn't know any better, so that's what happened to me. Joe was born groggy and sleepy, and he stayed that way for several days due to the drugs I had been given. I remember a nurse coming into my room and telling me that I had a boy. I looked at him in a fog, thought, "That's nice," and fell asleep again.

Nursing was less than successful right from the start. The nurses were very "helpful," bringing him out every four hours, and reassuring me that even though he wasn't nursing well, they were giving him formula in the nursery so he wouldn't starve! Big help!

We came home, after ten long days, with a fine supply of formula to get us started. We stayed at my mother's house, because Greg was in the Army and was only going to be home for a couple more days. I remember so well his disastrous attempts at mixing formula in my mother's kitchen, while the baby screamed, and I anxiously paced the bedroom floor. Poor Greg ended up breaking the big glass measuring cup, spilling the sticky stuff all over the floor, and finally giving up in despair while my long-suffering mother took over.

What with strict schedules, bottles after each nursing, and absolutely no encouragement (Greg now being on the high seas), nursing Joe soon came to an end.

Before Bill was born eighteen months later, Dr. Dick-Read had written his famous book. Greg brought it home one day and suggested I read it. We thought it made sense, and I agreed to "give it a try." So on a very hot August day in 1947, I went into labor. I remember sitting on our back porch, Tom Collins in hand, before starting off for the hospital. I remember carefully timing contractions, and writing it all down, and gamely pretending to read the *Ladies Home Journal* in between.

I did have a natural delivery, although I think I made the doctor very nervous. He had never worked on a conscious mother before and didn't know quite how to manage it. Greg managed to be a tactful go-between.

Well, I did nurse Bill with never a bottle in the house. In fact, after our first baby, I never gave any of them even one bottle from that time on. But Bill was a colicky baby. In fact, he was the most colicky baby I had ever heard of. He seemed to want to be nursed all the time, and nighttimes were especially awful. He was awake and screaming about every half-hour every night for seven months. The two of us paced the floor with him, I nursed him again and again, he would drop off to sleep, and I would ever so gently lay him in his crib. Then, bang, the minute I got back in bed, he would wake up, and the whole thing would start all over again. I have always had a positive dread of losing sleep, and of course things just went from bad to worse, as I got more tired and frazzled. But Greg kept encouraging me, and of course the baby gained hugely, as colicky babies so often do.

Our last hospital delivery was Peggy, born nineteen months after Bill. Then, before Katie was born, we learned that our obstetrician would be out of town. Greg must have suggested that we just stay home this time. Dr. Ratner, who had been one of Greg's teachers in medical school and was a longtime close friend, was willing to come out for the delivery. The labor progressed, with me comfortably ensconced in a rocking chair in the living room, while Greg and Herb talked shop endlessly (and I occasionally felt rather left out). Herb's wife Dorothy came over to lend a hand with the other children. Around two in the afternoon, I knew it wouldn't be much longer. I was only anxious that little Peggy, about nineteen months old, would go down for her nap before I had to be busy about other things, such as having a baby. Sure enough, she got sleepy soon after, and I recall carrying her upstairs, pausing for a contraction on the way, and tucking her into her crib. (My, those were the old days, weren't they?)

Dorothy Ratner took the boys out for a walk, and soon afterward, Katie arrived. We were all just delighted. When Dorothy brought the boys in I was waiting back in the rocking chair again, proudly holding the new little sister. But the boys had been promised a birthday party for the baby, so with scarcely a glance at her, they headed for the kitchen —"Where's the cake?"

And so it began. Anne came along two years later, and Jeannie two years and a day after that.

Michael was our first "League" baby, born in March of 1957. I had really been praying hard for another boy, after four girls, and after quite a long and difficult labor, because he was a face presentation, Michael arrived. He sure looked funny at first, since his face was a little battered by having replaced the back of his head as a battering ram. But he soon shaped up and is a handsome twenty-year-old today.

I'm sure that starting La Leche League was something we were all just ripe for back then. We had all discovered just how much joy there was in mothering our little ones, and what fun it was being with them and learning all about them. Having a big family just seemed the most logical and best thing to do. (It still does, to me.)

But there were times, of course, when not everything was perfect. I remember the day I had to take

Mary and Molly, 1967.

Jeannie, age two, contemplating the joys of summer on the Whites' back steps.

The Whites' first grandchild, Gregory, seventeen months, playing with the Whites' youngest, his Aunt Elizabeth, ten months.

Mary with four of her grandchildren — Patrick and baby Clare on the left (Katie's children); Paul and baby Sara on the right (Bill's children).

The White children in 1956 — Bill, Peggy and Joe; Anne, Jeannie and Katie.

The Gregory White family, 1976.

89

the children to the dentist right after school. Anne was about two and Jeannie was a brand new baby. We were a bit rushed, so I grabbed some tangerines for a snack, one for each, and hustled the children off in the car. As we drove I handed out the tangerines, one for Joe, one for Bill, and so on. When I got to "one for Anne," with my arm reaching over the back seat, there was no answer, and no one took the tangerine. "Where's Anne?" Suddenly, I realized that we had left her home! What a horrible moment. In my haste, and in my preoccupation not to forget the new baby, my quiet little two-year-old had been left behind. I drove frantically back home, and there she was, half-hiding behind the living room drapes, frightened and crying. I'll never forget that moment.

Through the next four years that we lived in Franklin Park after the League began, I remember being totally absorbed in mothering my children and in La Leche. Since the two were so intimately bound up with each other, it was hard to know where one began and the other left off.

Two and a half years after Michael was born, Mary, the last of our Franklin Park babies, was born. Mary was five months old when we moved a few miles away to River Forest, in January of 1960. Clare was born in September of 1962. Molly three years after that.

I had always said I'd love to have twelve children. I had at least a dozen names picked out from the time I was very young. Well, we got up to ten, and then as I passed my middle forties I figured that that was all the good Lord had in store for us. But such was not the case. Five years after Molly Elizabeth arrived. It was the shortest pregnancy I ever had. For the first three months I thought I was in the menopause! I was forty-seven when she was born, and it was the easiest labor and delivery of them all. Now our little Caboose, as my mother calls her, is six and in first grade.

But my theory of the ideal family situation has fulfilled itself in one way at least. I didn't want to have to cope with a Youngest Child, who would always be looked upon and treated as the baby and spoiled to death. I felt that by the time your youngest was outgrowing toddlerhood, the grandchildren should start coming along. And sure enough, we went one better than that. Our first grandson, Gregory Edmund White, was born at home on our third floor, delivered by his proud grandfather, seven months before his Aunt Elizabeth arrived on the scene (one floor below).

So today our children are grown or growing. Four of them are married, with nine children among them, and are the most wonderful parents in the world. I have a bearded husband (more than a bit grey by now), three bearded sons, and two bearded sons-in-law! Saves money on razor blades!

Our two oldest sons are now doctors, like their father, in family medicine. Bill is taking over some of the home deliveries, now so much in demand, and Joe is working primarily at one of the nearby hospitals. Joe and Bill married sisters, Susan and Cathy Dougherty. Joe and Susan have three children, Bill and Cathy have two children, as do Katie and Kevin Thorton and Jeannie and Jim Stirton.

And what of the other children now in 1977? Well, we still say we have eleven children, even though back in 1968 we lost our Peggy. She died at the age of eighteen of cancer. She was a real inspiration to everyone who knew her. She had her leg amputated when she was sixteen, but went ahead and ran for class president of her senior class. She won, and was very active in school affairs. She was a National Merit Scholar, and got the highest score possible on the English achievement test. She started her college career, even though she knew she could not have long to live. The cancer had spread to her lungs. She died after completing the first semester of her freshman year in college, and left behind a lovely collection of her writings; poems and essays about life—hers, ours, and God's wonderful world, which meant so much to her. "Celebrate Your Existence" was her philosophy, and she lived by that. Peggy is still very much with us today, and when things get tough, we recall how hard it was for her, and how beautifully she accepted all that was in store for her. I hope all mothers will Celebrate Their Existence, and that of their families.

Anne is an interpreter-translator for Lions International Clubs and travels all over the world in her job. Mike is a junior at St. John's College in Minnesota, and Mary is a freshman at St. Catherine's college in St. Paul, Minnesota. Clare is a freshman in high school, Molly in sixth grade, and Elizabeth in first.

And the League? I know it's influenced my life. As I meet more and more of the wonderful mothers who comprise League all over the world, I am constantly reinspired and recharged in my own mothering. My fellow founding mothers are some of the very finest women I could ever hope to meet, and I love them all dearly. The other mothers who have come with us in La Leche are just as fine, and it's the most wonderful feeling to know that wherever I go in the world, I will find someone whose name is familiar to me, and who will reflect the same values and the same principles of good mothering that I do.

As Dr. Ratner said in his Foreword to our manual, quoting Chesterton:

To be Queen Elizabeth within a definite area, deciding sales, banquets, labors and holidays; to be Whitely within a certain area, providing toys, boots, sheets, cakes and books; to be Aristotle within a certain area, teaching morals, manners, theology and hygiene: I can understand how this might exhaust the mind, but I cannot understand how it could narrow it. How can it be a large career to tell other people's children about the Rule of Three and a small career to tell one's own children about the universe. How can it be broad to be the same thing to everyone and narrow to be everything to someone. No, a woman's function is laborious, but because it is gigantic, not because it is minute.

There is no greater nor more challenging career than that of mothering. The rewards, when they come, are great indeed.

A Postscript To The Reader

More likely than not, you are someone who has been part of the story of La Leche League. Maybe you've found yourself mentioned in this long-awaited history, but more probably, you haven't.

As I began researching material for this book and interviewing the founding mothers, it quickly became apparent that there were more people who had made significant contributions of time and talent to the League than we could possibly do justice to in the space available.

Some of these people who were very active and very important in shaping the League's destiny became less active as they moved away or their children grew up and their interests turned to other things. Others have kept right on being active and interested in LLL.

But whether they have come and gone or are still around, there were just too many to even mention them all, let alone do justice to them!

When a more comprehensive history of the League is written someday, perhaps it will be possible to give proper credit to everyone who contributed to making La Leche League what it is.

"You'd never be able to get them all in, no matter how big a book you wrote," Marian said.

Probably we couldn't. But it would be fun to try.

Meanwhile, dear reader, whether your name appears in these pages or not, remember that this LLLove Story is really about you.

LLLove
Kaye Lowman

Notes and Autographs

Notes and Autographs

Notes and Autographs